The **ESSENTIALS** of

MONEY & BANKING I

John A. Naylor, Ph.D.

Chairperson and Professor, Department of Economics
Wabash College, Crawfordsville, IN

This book covers the usual course outline of Money &
Banking I. For related topics, see *"THE ESSENTIALS
OF MONEY & BANKING II."*

Research and Education Association
61 Ethel Road West
Piscataway, New Jersey 08854

THE ESSENTIALS®
OF MONEY & BANKING I

Printed in the United States of America

Library of Congress Catalog Card Number 95-68119

International Standard Book Number 0-87891-691-1

ESSENTIALS is a registered trademark of
Research & Education Association, Piscataway, New Jersey 08854

WHAT "THE ESSENTIALS" WILL DO FOR YOU

This book is a review and study guide. It is comprehensive and it is concise.

It helps in preparing for exams, in doing homework, and remains a handy reference source at all times.

It condenses the vast amount of detail characteristic of the subject matter and summarizes the **essentials** of the field.

It will thus save hours of study and preparation time.

The book provides quick access to the important facts, principles, theorems, concepts, and equations in the field.

Materials needed for exams can be reviewed in summary form – eliminating the need to read and re-read many pages of textbook and class notes. The summaries will even tend to bring detail to mind that had been previously read or noted.

This "ESSENTIALS" book has been prepared by an expert in the field, and has been carefully reviewed to assure accuracy and maximum usefulness.

Dr. Max Fogiel
Program Director

iii

CONTENTS

CHAPTER 1

MONEY AND FINANCIAL MARKETS

On any given weekday, an employee of the Federal Reserve Bank of New York will pick up the phone and call a government security dealer in New York and offer to buy or sell government securities. Within minutes the security dealer will close a deal with the Federal Reserve that will initially involve only the transfer of pieces of paper between the dealer and the Federal Reserve. Eventually, however, this seemingly sterile transfer will affect people across the United States, and may even have international repercussions. These transactions will affect the banking system, the money supply, interest rates, and eventually inflation and employment.

To understand why and how this chain of events occurs, we begin by explaining what money is, how it is measured and classified, and how it affects the economy. Next is an overview of the financial markets that both influence the creation of, and are affected by, the money supply. Subsequent chapters focus on the securities markets and financial intermediary markets that are involved in the transmission of monetary policy.

1.1 MONEY AND ITS MEASUREMENTS

1.1.1 DEFINING MONEY

Historically, many items such as feathers, sea shells, and precious metals have been used as money. Thus, history indicates that there is not a unique unit that is money. This leads economists not to define money in terms of a traditional unit, but as an abstract unit.

Money – economists view money as whatever performs the functions of money. The **money stock or money supply** is the amount of money in existence at a given point in time.

FUNCTIONS OF MONEY:

Medium of Exchange (widely accepted as payment for goods and services).

Unit of Account (the measure in which prices are denominated, e.g., the number of dollars per shirt).

Store of Value (maintains purchasing power over time).

Standard of Deferred Payments (the form in which future payments are denominated).

Money is not the same thing as **income** (earnings per time period) or **wealth** (the value of all property owned). Money is a **stock** that is measured at a point in time; income is a **flow** that is measured as an amount over a time period (such as a week or month). Someone with an income of $50,000 per year is not likely to have in hand $50,000 in money.

1.1.2 EMPIRICAL MEASURES OF THE MONEY SUPPLY

Because many assets provide some of the above functions to some degree, the actual measurement of the money supply is somewhat arbitrary. For the U.S., the Federal Reserve System publishes three widely used measures of the money supply, M1, M2, & M3.

M1 = Currency + Travelers' Checks + Transaction Deposits

M2 = M1 + Savings Deposits + Small Time Deposits + MMMF* +MMDA + Overnight RPS + Overnight Eurodollar Deposits

M3 =M2 + Large Time Deposits + Term RPs + Institutional MMMF + Term Eurodollar Deposits of U.S. Residents

*Excludes Institutional MMMF

Table 1.1
M1, M2, and M3 on February 20, 1989
Billions of Dollars

M1		**$ 771.1**
	Currency	$212.3
	Transactions Deposits	$551.5
	Travelers' Checks	$7.3
M2	M1 +	**$3061.3**
	Savings Deposits	$418.5
	Small Time Deposits	$1055.2
	MMMF	$248.8
	MMDA	$484.3
	Overnight RPs	$64.6
	Overnight Eurodollar Deposits	$18.8

M3	M2 +		$3937.1
	Large Time Deposits	$552.3	
	Term RPs	$129.2	
	Institutional MMMF	$ 89.0	
	Term Eurodollar Deposits	$105.3	

The following are definitions of the components of money measures:

Currency – sum of paper money and coins.

Transactions Deposits – deposits on which checks (or equivalent instruments) can be drawn without giving prior notice.

Time Deposits – interest bearing deposits that may be withdrawn only after a specified period of time.

Savings Deposits – interest bearing deposits that banks or savings institutions may require notice of up to 30 days before withdrawal. Most institutions waive the requirement in order to make the deposits attractive to customers.

MMMF (Money Market Mutual Funds) – shares in an investment company that invests only in short-term securities.

MMDA (Money Market Deposit Accounts) – time deposits on which a limited number of checks may be drawn.

RPs (Repurchase Agreements) – sale of a security which carries a promise by the seller to buy the security back the next day at a specified price.

Term RPs – RPs with a term before repurchase greater than one day.

4

Eurodollar Deposits – dollar denominated deposits of U.S. residents in banks outside of the U.S.

Federal Reserve System – quasi US governmental organization that is the central banking authority in charge of monetary policy.

The relative magnitudes of the three measures are given in Table 1.1.

1.1.3 MONEY CLASSIFICATIONS

Near Money: An asset that satisfies most, but not all, of the functions of money. The differences between M1 or M2 or M3 and many other financial assets are not distinct since many of the assets in M2 and M3 are not media of exchange but perform the other functions of money and are liquid. These highly liquid assets that are not media of exchange (such as Treasury Bills or CDs) are considered near monies.

Commodity Money: When a good such as gold or shells that has an intrinsic value is used directly or indirectly as money. When the commodity itself (e.g., gold coins) circulates as money, it is **full-bodied commodity money**. If a certificate fully redeemable for the commodity such as gold circulates, it is a **fully backed commodity money**. At one time, one dollar bills could be redeemed for silver coin whose silver content was worth $1 and hence the dollar bill was a fully backed commodity money. If the certificate used as money does not have a value in exchange equal to the commodity itself, it is **fractionally backed commodity money**. When five dollar bills were backed by about 25% of their value in gold, five dollar bills were fractionally backed commodity money.

Fiat Money: Money used in exchange that has little use as a commodity but is accepted because the government declares that it is money. If the government requires that the money be accepted in payments of debt, the government has declared that it is **legal tender**. In the U.S., since the government has determined that currency must be accepted in payment for debts, it has made currency a fiat money and legal tender. Fiat money may or may not be backed by a commodity such as gold; in the U.S., there once was, but no longer is, commodity backing for currency.

1.1.4 EFFECTS OF MONEY ON THE ECONOMY

1.1.4.1 MONEY AS A SOCIALLY PRODUCTIVE ASSET

The use of money enables a higher level of production and consumption by reducing inefficient bartering. In a barter economy, people spend more time:

arranging mutually acceptable trades,

analyzing a larger number of relative prices,

employing more middlepersons and traders.

The above activities use resources that could be used to produce more goods. Hence, the use of money frees resources for greater production.

1.1.4.2 MACROECONOMIC EFFECTS OF MONEY

Variations in the supply of money may affect the level of prices and output in the economy by influencing the demand for goods and services. **Monetary policy** affects the economy via the quantity of money and interest rates and is distinct from **fiscal policy**, which affects the economy via government expenditures and taxes.

1.2 INTRODUCTION TO FINANCIAL MARKETS

A financial market may be put into one of two major classifications:

Securities markets in which agents buy and sell the debt and equity claims of the ultimate borrowers. The markets in which the stocks of General Motors (an ultimate borrower) are bought and sold are security markets.

Financial intermediary markets in which agents trade in the claims of financial intermediaries. The market for savings deposits of commercial banks, for example, is a financial intermediary market. Financial intermediaries act as intermediaries in that they collect the funds of savers by issuing their own liabilities (e.g., savings deposits) and lending the funds to borrowers. This process is known as financial intermediation or indirect finance. If the saver purchases the debt of the borrower directly, direct finance (or nonintermediation) occurs.

Figure 1.1 illustrates the direct and indirect flows of funds from the saving units in the economy to the ultimate users of the funds. When funds flow through the upper path, financial intermediation occurs, while the funds flowing through the lower path provide direct finance.

The role of financial markets is to transfer funds from savers with excess funds to spenders with insufficient funds. This process permits funds to flow to the most productive uses of funds and consumers to achieve a more satisfactory consumption pattern over their lifetimes.

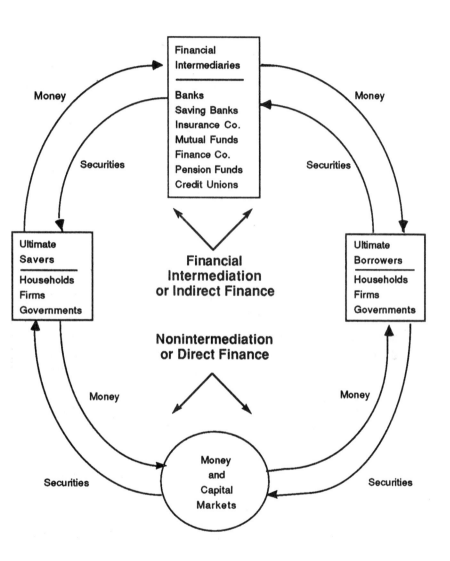

FIGURE 1.1–Intermediation and Nonintermediation

8

CHAPTER 2

SURVEY OF SECURITY MARKETS

To understand how banks operate and how monetary policy affects the economy, it is necessary to understand the nature of financial markets, the financial assets traded in these markets, and how interest rates are determined. This chapter describes the broad classifications of financial markets, describes the major financial assets traded in the money and capital markets, shows how various interest rates (yields) are computed, and identifies several common security market specialists.

2.1   TYPES OF FINANCIAL MARKETS AND INSTRUMENTS

Financial markets fall into one or more of the following contrasting pairs:

Debt vs. Equity Markets

Primary vs. Secondary Markets

Money vs. Capital Markets

Exchange vs. Over-the-counter Markets

Debt Market – a market in which securities evidencing promise to repay borrowed amounts plus interest are traded.

Equity Market – a market in which securities evidencing ownership rights are traded.

Primary Market – a market in which *new* securities are sold to the first buyers.

Secondary Market – a market in which securities are sold by the first and subsequent buyers; a market for secondhand securities.

Money Market – a market in which securities with initial maturities of less than one year are traded; a market for short-term securities such as Treasury Bills.

Capital Market – a market in which securities with more than one year (including equities) to maturity are traded; a market for intermediate and long-term securities such as 20 year government bonds and corporate common stock.

Exchanges – a secondary market in which the securities are traded in one central location such as the New York Stock Exchange.

Over-the-counter Market – a non-centralized, secondary market in which dealers at different locations stand ready to buy and sell securities from the dealer's inventories at prices quoted by the dealer. Large denomination certificates of deposit are not traded at one central location, but are traded at a number of large banks which are willing to buy or sell CDs of well-known banks. The secondary CD market is, thus, an over-the-counter-market.

10

2.1.1 FUNCTIONS OF THE MONEY AND CAPITAL MARKETS

They provide mechanisms that allow governments, consumers, and businesses to raise funds from economic agents with surplus funds within a short period at a relatively low cost.

They provide for an efficient means of allocating capital since borrowers with the most productive use of funds can bid for savings.

They integrate the banking system by enabling banks to bid for funds in all parts of the banking system.

2.2 MAJOR FINANCIAL MARKET INSTRUMENTS

2.2.1 TERMS USED IN IDENTIFYING FINANCIAL INSTRUMENTS

The terms "financial instrument", "financial claim", "financial asset" and "security" are used interchangeably. Securities sold in the above markets differ in maturity, risks, and rates of return, and may be sold at a premium or discount.

Maturity (Term to Maturity) – the time period, such as the number of years, until the face value is payable. A security whose face value will be paid ten years from now has a maturity of ten years.

Face Value (Par Value) – the amount promised to the holder at the maturity date of the bond or the nominal price of the security stated on the security. For example, a bond issued by Apple Computer Corporation that states on the bond that the owner will be paid $5000 in ten years has a face or par value of $5000.

Sold at a Discount – a sale of a security at a price less than the face or par value of the security. If an Apple Computer bond with a face value of $5000 sells for $4900, it sells at a discount.

Sold at a Premium – a sale of a security at a price greater than the face value of the security. If the $5000 Apple Computer bond sells for $5100, it sells at a premium.

Debt Security – the security itself is the written promise of the original issuer of the security (the borrower) to make payments of interest and principal at specified dates to the current owner of the security. A 20 year mortgage loan is a debt security in which the borrower promises to pay the bank interest and portions of the principal each month for the next 20 years. A debt security is merely a fancy IOU.

Equity Security – a security representing a claim to a portion of the net income of a firm and specified ownership rights such as voting at shareholder meetings. The common stock of IBM is an equity security.

2.2.2 MONEY MARKET INSTRUMENTS

Treasury Bill – a security issued by the U.S. Treasury with an original maturity of a year or less, promising to pay the bearer a fixed price (the face value) at maturity. Treasury bills are sold at a discount so that the income from the bills is the difference between the purchase price and the face value. You might pay $9800 for a Treasury bill maturing in 60 days with a face value of $10,000, yielding an income of $200.

(Prime) Commercial Paper – short-term, unsecured promissory notes sold at a discount by well known corporations with high credit standing. Instead of borrowing from banks for 90 days, Ford Motor Co. may sell its own notes (commercial paper) promising to pay the holders of the notes $1 million per note in 90 days, for example.

Bankers' Acceptance – a bank draft* originated by a firm, payable at a stated date that has been warranted by the bank when the bank stamps it "ACCEPTED". Typically the originating firm uses the draft to pay a foreign exporter for goods the firm wishes to import. Quality Coffee, for example, wishes to import $5 million in coffee beans from Columbia Exports. Rather than borrowing $5 million from First National Bank, Quality persuades Columbia to take a draft drawn on First National with a face value of $5.1 million maturing in 90 days. Columbia then presents the draft to First National for its acceptance. By accepting the draft (agreeing to pay the amount of the draft at maturity), the bank substitutes its credit rating for Quality Coffee's and receives a fee from Quality for doing so. Columbia Exports may hold the acceptance until its maturity date or sell it in the secondary market for acceptances. During the 90 days, Quality can process and sell the coffee beans and remit $5.1 million, plus a fee, to First National which uses the $5.1 million to pay the owners of the banker's acceptance at the end of 90 days. Quality Coffee would prefer this means of financing imports if the acceptance fee is less than an interest payment. Columbia Exports would prefer to have the banker's acceptance rather than an IOU from Quality Coffee if First National has a lower default risk than Quality Coffee. First National is able to earn income from the fee without employing its own funds (as long as Quality Coffee pays the $5.1 million plus the fee within 90 days).

---

* A draft instructs an agent to pay the owner of the draft a specified amount at a specified date. In the above example the draft instructs First National to pay the holder of the draft $5.1 million 90 days hence.

(Large Denomination Negotiable) Certificates of Deposit (CDs) – a marketable certificate for funds deposited at a bank, representing the bank's promise to pay the holder specified interest and the original amount of the deposit to the owner of the certificate. The "large" certificates sold in the money market have minimum units of $100,000. These are similar to the consumer CDs except that these are large denomination certificates and are negotiable with a ready market for resale because a number of large banks are prepared to buy and sell the large CDs from well known banks. General Motors, for example, might find the CD an attractive way to invest a billion dollars for 90 days because they know that if they should have an unexpected need for funds in the next 90 days, they could readily sell the CD in the secondary market.

Repurchase Agreement – a transaction in which agent A sells a security to agent B and agent B agrees to sell the security back to agent A at a specified time and price. It is essentially a loan by Agent B to agent A with the interest being the difference between the second and initial prices. Many repurchase agreements are between commercial banks and corporate clients. If CitiBank sells $1 million in Treasury bills to USX (U.S. Steel) and agrees to repurchase them in 5 days for $1.001 million, it is essentially a low risk method for U.S. Steel to invest $1 million since it does not face any chance of selling the T-bills at a price less than $1.001 million. CitiBank gains funds that it may invest in other assets.

(Negotiable) Eurodollar Deposit – a negotiable certificate of deposit for a dollar denominated deposit in a bank outside of the U.S. When IBM deposits $5 million in Barclays of London and the deposit is in terms of dollars, not pounds, it is a Eurodollar deposit.

Federal Funds – a loan made by one U.S. bank to another in which the transfer of funds is accomplished by instructing the Federal Reserve (FED) to transfer the appropriate amount of funds from the lending bank's account to the borrowing bank's account at the FED. The funds are immediately available to the borrowing bank, whereas funds raised by selling securities are not transferred for two days. For example, if NCNB lends $10 million in federal funds to Chase Manhattan for 1 day, NCNB would order the FED to transfer $10 million from NCNB's account *at the FED* to the account of Chase Manhattan at the FED. One day later, Chase Manhattan would instruct the FED to transfer the $10 million plus an interest payment from its FED account to the FED account of NCNB. Sometimes the term "federal funds" is used by bankers to refer to any immediately available funds.

2.2.3 CAPITAL MARKET INSTRUMENTS

Equities and intermediate and long-term debt are traded in the capital market. Intermediate-term debt has a maturity of 1 to 5 years, while long-term debt has a maturity of 5 or more years.

Bond − a debt security representing the claim to coupon (interest) payments at specified intervals and payment of the face or par value of the security at maturity.

Coupon − an interest payment, or in a literal sense, the piece of paper the bond holder sends to the bond issuer in order to claim the interest payment due.

A bond promising to pay the holder $100 each year for the next 20 years and $1000 at the end of 20 years has a coupon of $100, a face or par value of $1000, and a maturity of 20 years. The security's market price may be more or less than $1000.

Treasury Bond − a bond issued by the U.S. Treasury promising to pay interest at specified intervals (usually every six months) plus the face or par value of the security at maturity. Treasury bonds have an original maturity of over five years.

Treasury Note – same as a Treasury Bond except that the original maturity is between one and five years.

Corporate Bond – a bond issued by a corporation such as IBM promising to pay interest at specified intervals (usually every six months) and the par or face value at maturity.

Corporate Stock – an equity security issued by a corporation that entitles the holder to a share of dividends issued and may entitle the holder to vote at stockholders' meetings.

Consol – a bond promising to pay interest at certain dates but without a promise to pay the face value at any time (the maturity date is infinite).

2.3 ATTRIBUTES OF FINANCIAL INSTRUMENTS

A risk averse, wealth-seeking investor prefers financial instruments with high yields, high liquidity, high divisibility, low market risk, low default risk, and low transactions costs.

Yield – generally, the rate of return or the rate of interest on a security. Methods of calculating yields are given in 2.4 below.

Liquidity – the attribute of an asset that can be sold quickly and easily at a price close to its full value. Land is usually not a liquid asset because it is unlikely that it can be sold quickly on any given day at a price near the price achievable if a longer time to search for buyers were available. Treasury bills and

16

other money market instruments are liquid assets.

Market Risk (Interest Rate Risk) – the risk that the market price of the asset will decline as interest rates rise. Bond prices and interest rates, for example, typically vary hour by hour and day by day. When interest rates on bonds rise, bond prices fall.

Divisibility – the size of the units by which the instrument may be purchased. Money is divisible to 1 cent, so it is highly divisible. Treasury bills are less divisible as they have a minimum unit of $10,000.

Default Risk (Credit Risk) – the risk that the issuer of a security will fail to make the promised payments of interest or face value.

Transactions Cost – explicit and implicit costs of purchasing and selling securities, including search costs, costs of acquiring information about the likelihood of default, and brokerage costs.

Time Path of Payments – the pattern of interest and principal payments through time.

Present Value (PV) – today's value of an asset that generates a future stream of income. It is usually calculated by discounting the future stream of income (see below).

Future Value (FV) – the value at some future date an asset earning a specified rate of return would have. If $A are invested for N years earning a rate of return of i per year, the future value (FV) would be:

$$FV_N = A(1 + i)^N$$

17

If $1000 is invested in a CD at 10 percent for 5 years the future value would be:

$$FV_5 = 1000(1 + .10)^5 = 1000(1.61051) = 1610.51$$

2.4 CALCULATION OF INTEREST RATES (YIELDS) ON FINANCIAL ASSETS

2.4.1 SOME BASIC CONCEPTS

Discount Rate – the number d in the following formula that equates the right hand side with the **present value** (PV). It reflects the preference of an investor for currently available funds relative to future funds.

$$PV_t = \frac{C_t}{(1+d)^1} + \frac{C_{t+1}}{(1+d)^2} + \ldots + \frac{C_{t+N}}{(1+d)^N}$$

where C_{t+i} is the amount paid in year $(t + i)$ to the owner of the asset.

If Jane feels that $100 today is just as satisfactory as $110 one year in the future, the present value of $110 for Jane would be $100 and Jane's discount rate would be 10% since $100 = 110/(1 + d)$ implies that $d = .10$. If Jane feels that $110 one year into the future is worth only $90 (PV=90), her discount rate is .22.

Interest Rate or Yield – a measure of the rate of return earned on an asset. Unless qualified, the interest rate refers to the yield to maturity on an asset.

2.4.2 COMMONLY QUOTED INTEREST RATE MEASURES

Yield to maturity – the average annual rate of return if an asset is held to its maturity. It reflects both the interest payments and the capital gain or loss. It is the yield typically quoted; in most cases "the interest rate" is understood to mean the yield to maturity. For a bond with a market price of P that promises to pay $C once each year for the next N years plus a final payment (face value or par value) of F at the end of the Nth year, the yield to maturity is the number r in the following:

$$P = \frac{C}{(1+r)^1} + \frac{C}{(1+r)^2} + \ldots + \frac{C}{(1+r)^N} + \frac{F}{(1+r)^N}$$

Suppose FINCORP issues a bond promising to pay $20 interest at the end of each year for the next 3 years and $500 after 3 years, and the market price of the bond is $490. The yield to maturity is 5.065% since

$$490 = \frac{20}{(1+r)^1} + \frac{20}{(1+r)^2} + \frac{20}{(1+r)^3} + \frac{500}{(1+r)^3}$$

implies that $r = .05065$.

The yield to maturity can be approximated by $r = \{[C + (F - P)/N]/P\}$. In the FINCORP example the approximation of the yield is $r = \{[20 + (500 - 490)/3]/490 = .0476$. The approximation formula is used when a book of yields or computer calculation is not available.

Current Yield – the ratio $(100C/P)$; a crude measure of the interest flow per dollar invested. For FINCORP, the current yield is 4.08% [$=100(20/490)$] indicating that each dollar invested earns about 4.08 cents per year.

19

Nominal Yield (Nominal Rate or Coupon Rate) – the ratio ($100C/F$); this measure is used to compare the interest flow per bond. For FINCORP the nominal yield would be 4% [$=100(20/500)$], indicating that each dollar of face value pays 4 cents per year in interest.

Holding period yield – the rate of return earned over the actual time that the security is held. The yield to maturity assumes that the security is held until maturity,which is often not the case. For a security with an annual coupon payment of $\$C$, purchased for $\$P$, and sold for $\$S$ after M years, the holding period yield is the number h below

$$P = \frac{C}{(1+h)^1} + \frac{C}{(1+h)^2} + \dots + \frac{C}{(1+h)^M} + \frac{S}{(1+h)^M}$$

Approximation formula: $h = [\,C + (S-P)/M\,]\,/P$

If a bond with a $100 coupon was purchased for $9500 and was sold after one year for $9555, the holding period yield would be 1.631% since

$$\$9500 = \frac{100}{(1+h)^1} + \frac{9555}{(1+h)^1}$$

implies that $h = .01631$. In this case, the actual and approximation formulas for the holding period yield provide the same answer because $M = 1$. S may be equal to, less than, or greater than F, and M is less than N.

For a security held for D days ($D \le 365$), h is calculated as:

$$h = [(365/D)\,(S+C-P)]/P$$

The holding period yield for a bond purchased for $990, with a coupon of 50, held for 90 days, and sold for $995 would be 22.53% since

$$h = [(365/90)\ (995 + 50 - 990)]/990 = .2253$$

Discount Yield (yield on a discount basis) – Dealers in the Treasury bill market quote yields as the discount yield (r_{db}) calculated as:

$$r_{db} = \frac{(F - P)}{F}\ \frac{(360)}{D}$$

where F is the par or face value of the Treasury bill, P is the market price of the bill, and D is the number of days to maturity $(D \leq 365)$. A 90 day Treasury bill with a market price of $9,800 and a face value of $10,000 would have a discount yield of 8% since

$$r_{db} = \frac{(10,000 - 9,800)}{10,000}\ \frac{(360)}{90} = .08$$

The discount yield understates the true yield to maturity because of the assumption that the year is 360 days long and because it uses the par value rather than the market price in the denominator. The true yield for the above example would be 8.28%, since using the holding period yield formula for a 90 day holding period gives:

$$h = \frac{(10,000 - 9,800)}{10,000}\ \frac{(365)}{90} = .0828$$

Capital Gain – the difference between the price of an asset when sold, S, and its purchase price, P. When the difference is negative it is a capital loss. If a bond is purchased for $990 and sold for $995, the capital gain is $5 = 995 - 990$.

21

Rate of Capital Gain (g) – the capital gain expressed as an annual percent of the purchase price, P.

$$g = \frac{100(365)\,(S - P)}{D(P)}$$

where D = number of days the security is held; S = sales price; P = purchase price.

If a bond were purchased for \$5000 and sold 5 days later for \$5050, the rate of capital gain would be 73% since

$$g = \frac{100(365)\,(5050 - 5000)}{5(5000)} = 73\%$$

2.5   IMPORTANT FACTS ABOUT SECURITY YIELDS AND PRICES

The above mathematics of yields implies two key facts about the relationships between bonds and yields:

The price of a bond and the yield-to-maturity are inversely related. If the bond price falls, the yield rises (See Figure 2.1).

For a given change in the level of interest rates, the price of longer-term bonds will be greater than the price of shorter-term securities.

Historical Data show the following patterns:

Long-term bond prices have varied more than short-term security prices; see Figure 2.2.

Short-term security yields vary more than long-term yields; see Figure 2.3.

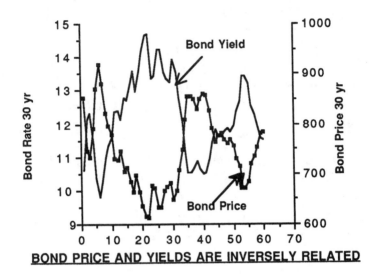

BOND PRICE AND YIELDS ARE INVERSELY RELATED

FIGURE 2.1–1980 – 85   30 Year Treasury Bond Prices
and Yields

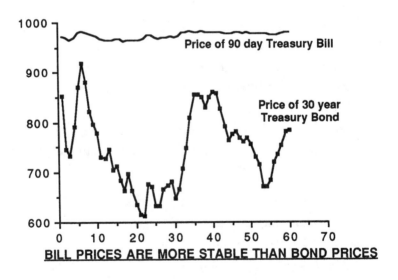

BILL PRICES ARE MORE STABLE THAN BOND PRICES

FIGURE 2.2–1980–85 Treasury Bill and Bond Prices

23

All interest rates tend to move up and down together (but not in an exact lockstep) during expansions and contractions in economic activity.

2.6 SECURITIES MARKET SPECIALISTS

Most buyers and sellers of securities utilize the services of securities specialists in making their securities transactions. The more prominent specialists are cited below.

Investment Bankers – agents that acquire new security issues and sell them to investors. They may purchase a new issue on their own account or contract to sell the securities for a fee. The security issuer may choose to place the new securities with an investment banker rather than selling the whole issue on the retail market and risking the possibility that such a large placement would result in a low price for the security. In the recent corporate takeovers, the investment banks were the specialists who (on behalf of the takeover group) sold the high risk

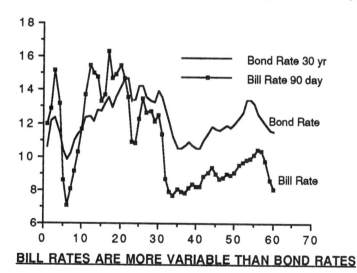

BILL RATES ARE MORE VARIABLE THAN BOND RATES

FIGURE 2.3–1980 – 85: 90-day Bill Rate and 30-Year Bond Rate ("junk") bonds piecemeal to various investors rather than having the takeover group place the entire issue up for sale at one time.

Securities Brokers – agents who sell or buy securities on behalf of clients for a fee. Because of their knowledge of potential buyers and sellers, brokers may be better able to match buyers and sellers than individual agents might on their own.

Securities Dealers – agents who buy securities for their own inventory and sell securities from their own inventory of securities. The "**bid price**" is the price the dealer offers to pay and the "**ask price**" is the price the dealer offers to sell at. Dealers earn income from the difference between the ask and bid prices.

CHAPTER 3

INTEREST RATE DETERMINATION

A glance at the financial pages of a newspaper will quickly verify that there are thousands of interest rates on a wide variety of securities. In this chapter, we outline the factors that affect the level of the average interest rate at different points in time, and the factors responsible for differences in interest rates on various securities at the same point in time. The analysis of these two issues requires insight on the portfolio choices of investors. Hence, we begin by a quick review of the investor **portfolio choice**, decisions that investors make in allocating their wealth among various assets (3.1). We then consider the factors affecting the level of interest rates at different points in time (3.2), and end by examining the factors responsible for the structure of interest rates at any point in time (3.3).

3.1 INTRODUCTION TO PORTFOLIO CHOICE

Investors' selection of securities depends on
the investor attitudes towards risk,

the investor perception of the risks of various securities,
and

the expected rates of return on securities.

Investors may be risk averse, risk neutral, or risk loving. A **risk averse** investor prefers a certain income of $10 to a 10% chance of getting $100. A **risk loving** investor gains satisfaction by undertaking more risk and would prefer a 10% chance of earning $100 over a guaranteed $10. A **risk neutral** investor is unconcerned with the risk and considers only the expected return; hence the risk neutral investor is indifferent between a certain $10 and a 10% chance of earning $100. **Indifference curves** showing the relationship between risk and expected return for the three types of investors are given in Figure 3.1. Each indifference curve shows the various combinations of risk and expected return that the investor finds equally satisfactory; higher indifference curves represent more preferred combinations.

The **Expected Return** refers to the mathematical expectation of the rate of return. It is a weighted average of the possible returns with the weights being the probability of the return occurring. For example, if there is a 20% chance of the

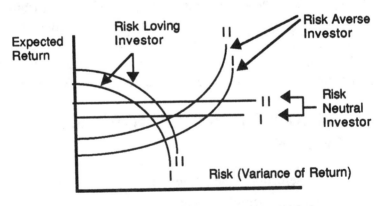

FIGURE 3.1–Indifference Curves for Three Types of Investors

27

return being 5%, 65% chance of it being 6% and a 15% chance of it being 4%, the expected return is 5.5%, since:

Expected Return = .2(5) + .65(6) + .15(4) = 5.5%.

If you can earn $1 on a coin toss if it is heads and $2 if it is tails, your expected return is $1.5 = .5($1) + .5($2).

The typical investor is risk averse; hence the investor's demand for a security will vary *positively* with its (1) expected return, (2) liquidity, and (3) wealth, and will vary *negatively* with the (1) riskiness of the asset and the (2) expected return on other assets. Investors select the combinations of assets (portfolios) that provide them with the most satisfactory mix of expected returns and risk. The potential amounts of each asset that the investor would purchase for her portfolio constitutes the investor's **demand of the asset.**

For a risk averse investor the demand for bond B is given in Figure 3.2 as D_o. The greater the interest paid on the bonds, *cet. par.*, the greater the expected return on the security. The higher expected return compensates investors for accepting the risks involved in owning the bond. Hence, an increase in the interest rate leads to an increase in the quantity of bonds demanded, producing a positively sloped demand curve. If investor wealth

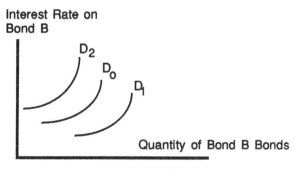

FIGURE 3.2–Demand for Bond B

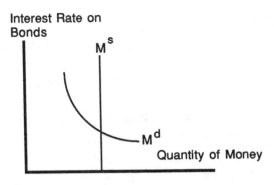

FIGURE 3.3–Interest Rate Level Determined by the Demand & Supply of Money

or the liquidity of bond B rises, the demand would shift to D_1. If the return on another security, e.g., bond C, rises or bond B becomes more risky, the demand would shift to D_2.

3.2 DETERMINATION OF THE LEVEL OF INTEREST RATES

3.2.1 LIQUIDITY PREFERENCE APPROACH

One approach to explaining the level of interest rates is the **liquidity preference approach**. For ease of analysis, since the principle is the same if thousands of assets are considered, we group all risky and interest earning assets into an asset called bonds so that the investor must select a portfolio consisting of a risky asset (bonds) and a safe but liquid asset (money). Finally, it is assumed that the investor possesses a given amount of total wealth which she is to allocate between bonds and money so as to gain the best mix of risk and return. The portfolio choice framework in the previous section implies that the demand for the risky asset, bonds, will be an upward sloping curve as in Figure 3.2. The demand for money reflects the investor preference for liquidity; since we are ignoring default risk, a preference for liquidity is a preference for low risk. The demand for money slopes downward because the lower the interest rate, the

29

lower the expected return on bonds and hence the smaller the quantity of bonds demanded. Since the investor's total wealth is fixed, a decrease in the investment in one asset implies an increase in the quantity demanded of the remaining assets including money. Another way of expressing the relationship is to say that the interest rate reflects the opportunity cost of holding low risk, but non-interest (or lower interest) bearing money balances. Given the supply of money, M^s, the level of interest rates will be determined by the intersection of the demand for money, M^d, and the supply of money (see Figure 3.3). The greater the public's preference for liquidity (the greater their aversion to the risk in bonds), the greater the demand for money (the further M^d will be to the right in Figure 3.3).

Factors Leading to Higher Interest Rates: A decrease in the supply of money or an increase in the demand for money will cause the level of interest rates to rise. The following will cause the money demand curve to increase (shift outward):

an increase in income,

an increase in wealth,

an increase in riskiness of bonds,

an increase in preference for liquidity,

an increase in the price level,

an increase in the expected rate of inflation, and

an increase in the supply of bonds.

3.2.2 LOANABLE FUNDS APPROACH

While the liquidity preference approach focuses on the demand for liquidity and hence on the demand for specific assets, an alternative but consistent approach is to view the level of interest rates as being the outcome of the demand and supply of loanable funds. The **demand for loanable funds** is the total quantity of funds borrowers wish to borrow at the various possible interest rates. It is the sum of the demands for borrowed funds or credit demand by households (C_{cr}), firms (B_{cr}), and governments (Gdef) plus the increase in the demand for money (ΔM^d). The combined deficits of state, local and federal governments (Gdef) is the demand for loanable funds by the government sector. In Figure 3.4, the middle panel illustrates the summation of the sector demands for loanable funds to obtain the total demand for loanable funds, D.

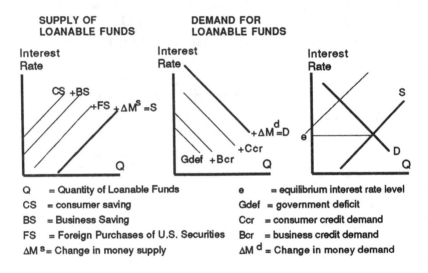

SUPPLY OF
LOANABLE FUNDS

DEMAND FOR
LOANABLE FUNDS

Q = Quantity of Loanable Funds	e = equilibrium interest rate level
CS = consumer saving	Gdef = government deficit
BS = Business Saving	Ccr = consumer credit demand
FS = Foreign Purchases of U.S. Securities	Bcr = business credit demand
ΔM^s = Change in money supply	ΔM^d = Change in money demand

FIGURE 3.4–Demand and Supply of Loanable Funds

The **supply of loanable funds** is the sum of household savings (CS), government savings (GS), and business savings (BS) plus the increase in the supply of money (ΔM^s), and inflows of capital from foreign countries (FS). The left panel in Figure 3.4 illustrates the summation of the sector supplies of loanable funds to obtain the total supply of loanable funds, S.

The **equilibrium level of the interest rate**, e, is at the intersection of the   demand for and supply of loanable funds.

31

Any factor increasing the supply of loanable funds or decreasing the demand for loanable funds decreases the interest rate. For example, a decrease in federal government expenditures decreases the deficit and hence decreases the demand for loanable funds and the rate of interest. An increase in the marginal propensity to save or an increase in income increases consumer saving and hence decreases the rate of interest.

The analyses produced by the liquidity preference and loanable funds frameworks give the same results and are consistent, alternative methods of analysis. To see the connection, note that an increase in the demand for loanable funds by a corporation will be achieved by an increase in the supply of bonds or other debt by the corporation. Similarly, if you save more of your income and invest the savings, in the loanable funds framework, the supply of loanable funds increases and the interest rate decreases. In the liquidity preference framework, your increased savings results in an increase in the demand for another asset such as bonds and a decrease in money demand so that the interest rate declines.

3.2.3 IMPACT OF EXPECTED INFLATION

The role of inflation expectations in the determination of the level of interest rates merits emphasis. When borrowers expect the rate of inflation to increase, their demand for loanable funds increases because firms will anticipate being able to sell goods at higher prices and hence will seek to borrow more at each rate of interest in order to finance expanded production. Borrowers in general expect to repay loans with dollars of lower purchasing power and thus the demand for loanable funds will shift vertically. Lenders expecting a higher rate of inflation, however, will recognize that the interest and principal repayments will yield less purchasing power than before and will not want to supply as many loanable funds at each interest rate as before. Hence an increase in the expected rate of inflation will lead to a decrease in the supply of loanable funds and an increase in the demand for loanable funds, producing a higher rate of interest.

If taxes are ignored and all economic agents have identical inflation expectations, a change in the expected rate of inflation will produce an equal change in the rate of interest. This proposition is known as the **Fisher Effect**.

The Fisher Effect may be expressed as: $r = i_{real} + \pi$ where r is the nominal interest rate, i_{real} is the real rate of interest and π is the expected rate of inflation. For example, according to the Fisher Effect proposition, if the real rate is 6% and the expected rate of inflation is 0%, the nominal rate should be 6%, but if the expected rate of inflation rises to 2%, the nominal rate should be 8%.

If interest is taxed, interest rates will change by more than the change in the expected rate of inflation in order that the real after-tax interest income per dollar be constant. Note, however, that if borrowers and lenders have different inflation expectations, rates may change by more or less than the change in the expected rate of inflation.

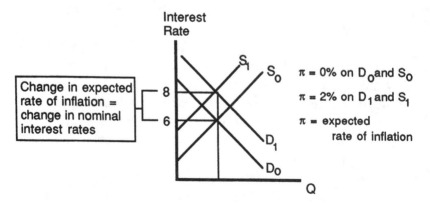

FIGURE 3.5–Fisher Effect

33

Does an increase in the supply of money lower interest rates? The loanable funds and liquidity preference analysis seems to imply that there should be a decline in the level of interest rates if all else remains the same. Note that in an expanding economy, the initial decline in interest rates due to an increase in the money supply (sometimes called the **liquidity effect**) may be subsequently offset by the increase in the demand for funds as real income rises (the **income effect**). In addition, if the level of prices rises, the amount of nominal money demanded and the amount of loanable funds demanded will rise leading to a further increase in interest rates (the **price level effect or Keynes effect**). These two effects along with the Fisher Effect push interest rates in the opposite direction than the liquidity effect so that eventually the rise in the money supply may not cause a permanent decline in interest rates.

3.3 DETERMINATION OF THE STRUCTURES OF INTEREST RATES

The loanable funds and liquidity preference theories explain why average interest rate levels rise and fall but they do not explain why, at any point in time, interest rates on various debt instruments differ from one another. The patterns or structures of interest rates, at a point in time, can be attributed to differences in default risk, tax treatment, market risk, and expectations about future interest rate levels.

3.3.1 DEFAULT STRUCTURE OF INTEREST RATES

Securities with all characteristics the same except that they have different perceived default risks will have different interest rates. An AAA bond (the lowest default risk bond and thus the highest quality bond) has a lower interest rate than a D (the highest default risk and thus lowest quality) bond. The debt instruments of the U.S. government bear lower interest rates than corporate, state, or local government securities because the U.S. government has the power to tax and to issue currency if required to pay interest and principal on its debt. For these reasons, the U.S. government debt is perceived to have no default risk.

The Standard and Poor's bond rating scheme has nine rating categories of bond quality: AAA, AA, A, BBB, BB, B, CCC-CC, C, and D. The AAA bonds bear the lowest interest rates because they are perceived as having the lowest probability of default. The interest rates rise as one moves from AAA to AA, to A, etc. as the estimated risk of default rises. The higher rates on lower quality bonds provide compensation for the higher default risk.

3.3.2 TAX STRUCTURE OF INTEREST RATES

Interest rates vary on securities with equal characteristics except for tax treatment. An AAA rated ten year municipal bond will carry a lower interest rate than an AAA rated ten year corporate bond because the investor need not include the interest on most municipal bonds in his/her taxable income for federal income tax purposes. If securities X and Y are identical except that security X is taxed at a rate of t per year while security Y's interest is not taxed, the equilibrium relationship between the interest rate on X, r_x, and the rate on Y, r_y is expected to be:

$$r_y = r_x(1-t).$$

For example, if Y is an Indiana AAA, ten year bond, X is an AAA, ten year General Motors bond yielding 10%, and the marginal tax rate is 33%, r_y would be 6.7% since $r_y = 10(1 - .33) = 10(.67) = 6.7$. If this were not true, securities with the same risks would have different after-tax yields which is inconsistent with the notion that economic agents maximize net income.

When capital gains are taxed at a different rate than interest income, securities with different coupons will have different pretax interest rates. Bond II, a one year, AAA rated IBM bond with a 10% coupon, will have a higher yield than Bond I, a one year, AAA rated IBM bond with a 5% coupon, if the capital gains tax is lower than the tax on interest income. If this were not the case, the two equivalent securities would have unequal after-tax incomes resulting in an ignored profit opportunity.

For example, if the face value of each security is $100, IBM security I sells for $80, IBM Security II sells for $94.814, interest income is taxed at a 50% rate and capital gains are taxed at a 25% rate, both of the one year securities will have an after tax rate of return of 9.375%, but Security I will have a pretax rate of return of 31.25% while Security II will have a pretax rate of return of 16%. The computation of the after tax returns is given by:

After-tax rate of return I:

$$\frac{C(1-.5)+(F-P)(1-.25)}{P} =$$

$$\frac{10(.5)+(100-94.814)(.25)}{94.814} = .09375$$

After-tax rate of return II:

$$\frac{C(1-.5)+(F-P)(1-.25)}{P} =$$

$$\frac{10(.5)+(100-80)(.25)}{80} = .09375$$

The pretax rates of return are calculated with the yield to maturity formula in Chapter 2 for $N=1$.

3.3.3 TERM STRUCTURE OF INTEREST RATES

Even if all differences in tax treatment and default risk were accounted for, the remaining interest rates are still rarely equal. Instead, one typically observes that interest rates vary with the term to maturity of the securities. The relationship between the yield or interest rate on securities and their respective terms to maturity is known as the **term structure of interest rates** or the **yield curve.**

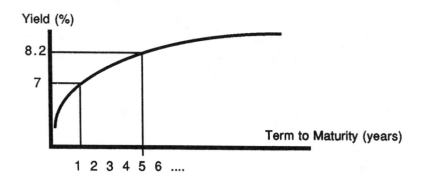

FIGURE 3.6–Term Structure of Interest Rates or Yield Curve

The shape of the yield curve is determined by the demand and supply for securities of different maturities. There are several rival theories as to what factors underlie the demands and supplies of securities of varying maturities. The **(Pure) Expectations Theory** assumes that investors are risk neutral investors seeking to maximize their wealth. Since such investors sell securities expected to yield less and buy securities expected to yield more over the planning horizon, this theory predicts that long-term rates will become averages of expected short-term securities. For example, if the investor knows that today's 1 year rate is 5% and expects the 1 year rate to be 7% next year, the pure expectations theory holds that the investor would not invest in a two year security unless it also would produce a value of $1.1235 or more in two years for each dollar invested now. This proposition can be demonstrated by noting that if you invest $1 for the first year at 5%, you would receive $1.05 at the end of one year. When you invest $1.05 at 7% for the second year, you would receive $1.1235 at the end of two years. If investing in the two year security is to yield at least the same future value as investing in a one year security in each of two years, the rate on a 2 year security must be 5.995% or more. Using the yield to maturity formula in Chapter 2, we see that investing $1 to get a future value of $1.1235 implies a yield of 5.995% which is the geometric average of 5% and 7%.

In general, the pure expectations theory concludes that the rate on a zero coupon, N-year security, R_N, is related to the expected one year rates for years 1, 2, ..., N $(r_1, r_2, ..., r_N)$ by the following:

$$(1 + R_N) = [(1 + r_1)(1 + r_2) ... (1 + r_N)]^{1/N}$$

That is, the theory implies that long-term rates are (geometric) averages of expected short-term rates. Hence, if investors expect rates to rise (fall) in the future, the yield curve will be positively (negatively) sloped, and if interest rates are expected to be unchanged in the future, the yield curve will be horizontal.

Some authors employ the following formula as an approximation to the geometric average:

$$R_N = [r_1 + r_2 + r_3 + ... + r_N]/N.$$

The pure expectations theory implies that investors are unaffected by the fact that their forecasts are often inaccurate and that short-term bonds have a smaller interest rate risk (less price variability) than long-term bonds. The **risk premium** or

liquidity preference theory holds that in view of the greater risk on longer-term securities, investors will hold the more risky securities only if they are compensated for the greater interest rate risk by a higher yield. This implies that long-term interest rates will be averages of the expected short-term rates plus a risk (liquidity) premium, L_N.

$$(1 + R_N) = [(1 + r_1) (1 + r_2) \ldots (1 + r_N)]^{1/N} + L_N$$

Thus, the risk premium theory implies that if interest rates are expected to be constant or rising, the yield curve (term structure of interest rates) will be positively sloped. The yield curve will be negatively sloped only if interest rates are expected to fall sharply enough to offset the liquidity premiums.

The risk premium theory implies that the only risk of concern to investors is the interest rate risk, but in some cases this is incorrect. For example, an investor that plans on living off of the interest payments may be more concerned with the certainty of the interest payments than the variability of the market price of the asset. In this situation, investing in a 20 year bond with a known coupon would be preferable to investing in a 1 year bond and planning on investing in 19 future 1 year bonds even if the average of the expected 1 year rates exceeded the yield on the 20 year bond. Similarly, a corporation planning on borrowing funds for five years may prefer to issue a five year bond to lock in the cost of the debt even if the five year yield exceeded that of the average of the expected 1 year yields. The **preferred habitat theory** of the term structure maintains that borrowers and lenders have preferred maturities and will move to other maturities only if the expectations of future rates imply a significantly large incentive to shift from the preferred maturity (habitat). Hence this theory holds that the shape of the yield curve depends on the distribution of preferred habitats among lenders and borrowers and upon expectations of future rates.

The **market segmentation theory** assumes that the maturity preferences are so important to investors that expectations about future rates are unimportant in the portfolio choices of investors. Hence, an upward sloping yield curve does not imply anything about interest rate expectations to market segmentation theorists. Rather, it simply implies that at that point in time, investors with a preference for short-term securities were more dominant in the bond market than investors preferring long-term securities.

CHAPTER 4

FINANCIAL INTERMEDIATION IN THE UNITED STATES

This chapter begins by indicating the primary function of financial intermediaries and explains why intermediaries have been able to attract the funds to perform a role. Next, the major types of intermediaries are described with an emphasis on the sources of funds and the types of assets in which the funds are invested. For this reason, they are categorized as depository and non-depository institutions. An overview of the regulatory structure of the intermediaries and programs designed to support the housing market concludes the chapter.

4.1 FUNCTION OF FINANCIAL INTERMEDIARIES

As indicated in Chapter 1, financial intermediaries facilitate the flow of funds between the savers and ultimate borrowers in the economy. If there were no intermediaries, individual savers would have to directly purchase the securities of borrowers. Without intermediaries, these **difficulties associated with direct contracting between lenders and borrowers** are more severe and inhibit the channelling of funds from savers to borrowers:

High information and search costs for bilateral loans.

Incompatibility of the maturity needs of lenders and borrowers since most savers want to lend funds at short maturities, while borrowers want to borrow at longer maturities.

Small amounts of individual savings do not match the larger loan amounts desired by borrowers.

Financial intermediaries issue their own debt claims to the saver in forms more attractive to savers, and in turn, lend to borrowers on terms satisfactory to the borrowers.

For the saver, the following are **advantages of** *depository* **intermediary claims:**

No market risk; a dollar deposited in a checking account, for example, is not redeemed at less than a dollar when interest rates rise.

Low default risk due to government agency backed insurance.

Wide choice of maturities on claims.

Low information and transactions costs.

The **primary disadvantages of depository claims** are:

The long run gross return may be lower than on direct investment.

Low inflation protection.

For *mutual funds* **the following characteristics are attractive to the saver:**

Professional management of funds.

Diversification and risk pooling.

High liquidity.

Rates of return close to those earned by direct investment in securities.

Low transaction costs.

By virtue of their large scale of investment activity and due to specialization, financial intermediaries achieve (relative to an individual's direct purchase of securities) the following:

Low information and transaction costs.

High liquidity.

Lower risk per dollar of investment.

These factors enable the intermediaries to achieve a better risk-return combination than small investors. Thus, they are able to issue their own claims (such as certificates of deposit or money market mutual fund shares) to savers that offer risk and return characteristics more attractive than direct investment by the savers. As a consequence, there has been a rapid growth in the volume and variety of financial intermediaries. The main intermediaries will be described below.

4.2 DEPOSITORY INSTITUTIONS

4.2.1 COMMERCIAL BANKS

The approximately 15,000 commercial banks comprise one of the most dominant financial institutions in the U.S. Table 4.1 shows that they have over double the assets of the next class of institutions.

Table 4.1
Total Assets of Major Financial Intermediaries

Intermediary	Total Assets*
Commercial Banks	$2,857
Savings and Loan Associations	1,263
Mutual Savings Banks	259
Credit Unions	183
Life Insurance Companies	1,006
Fire & Casualty Insurance Co.	386
Finance Companies	394
Investment Companies	789

*December 1987 in billions of $. Source: 1988 Mutual Fund Fact Book

Commercial banks are one of the most diversified financial intermediaries. The range of activities of commercial banks and bank holding companies will be discussed in detail in Chapter 5. For now, it is noted that commercial banks (ignoring the bank holding companies discussed in the next chapter) primarily raise funds from checking and savings deposits, while investing in consumer, business and mortgage loans, and securities of governments.

4.2.2 SAVINGS AND LOAN ASSOCIATIONS

Savings and Loan Associations, second in size in terms of total assets to commercial banks, number approximately 4,000. The savings and loans initially were formed under legislation designed to increase the flow of savings into home mortgage lending. Although recently the restrictions on investments by savings and loans have been reduced, the savings and loans still invest the majority of their funds in home mortgages as shown in Table 4.2.

Table 4.2
Total Assets and Liabilities
of Savings and Loan Associations*

Assets

	$Billions	%
Mortgages	$707.6	56.0
U.S. Government Securities	218.9	17.3
Consumer Credit	41.3	3.3
Open Market Paper	23.4	1.9
Demand Deposits and Currency	15.0	1.2
Time Deposits	7.3	.5
Federal Funds + RPs	27.3	2.2
Miscellaneous	222.1	15.4
Total	$1,262.9	100.0

Liabilities

	$Billions	%
Deposits	$927.2	76.1
Federal Home Loan Bank Loans	141.6	11.6
Federal Funds and Repurchase Agreements	84.7	7.0
Bank Loans	31.9	2.6
Corporate Bonds	15.9	1.3
Miscellaneous	16.2	1.3
Total	$1,217.9	100.0

*September 1988

Because of the short maturity of their deposit liabilities and long maturity of their mortgage assets, savings and loans experienced major financial stress when interest rates rose sharply in the late 1970s and early 1980s. This was exacerbated by regulations restricting the interest the institutions could pay on their deposits. The rise in market rates relative to the rates paid by the **thrifts** (mutual savings banks, savings and loan associations, and credit unions) led to **disintermediation** as customers withdrew funds in order to invest in higher yield money market securities. Deregulation of the interest rates payable in the 1980s enabled the thrifts to compete for funds, but due to the maturity mismatch, the cost of funds exceeded the interest earned on investments. Undercapitalization, lack of diversification, and the difficulties facing managers in competing with commercial banks (who had greater experience in consumer and business lending) endangered many thrifts. The failure rate on savings and loans increased dramatically and remains a problem today.

4.2.3 MUTUAL SAVINGS BANKS

Mutual savings banks, with assets totalling $258.5 billion in November 1988, number about 400 and are located in the northeastern part of the United States. They are essentially of the same character as savings and loan associations. The term "mutual" indicates that they are owned by the depositors. With over 80% of their funds coming from deposits and about 50% of their assets invested in mortgage loans, the mutual savings banks faced the same problems and fate as the savings and loan associations.

4.2.4 CREDIT UNIONS

Credit unions are similar to mutual savings banks in that they are owned by their shareholders, but unlike mutual savings banks, the credit unions invest primarily in consumer loans made to members. Income of credit unions is distributed to members in proportion to their shares, like depositors in mutual savings banks. Shares may be thought of as deposits except for some legal technicalities.

4.3 NONDEPOSITORY FINANCIAL INTERMEDIARIES

4.3.1 INSURANCE COMPANIES

4.3.1.1 LIFE INSURANCE COMPANIES

In a competitive market, the premium paid for term life insurance is on average just sufficient to enable the insurance company to make the promised payment in the event of the death of the insured. The premium on whole or ordinary life insurance policies, on average, exceeds the amount needed to pay for death benefits. The amount of the premium in excess of the amount needed to pay death benefits is a form of savings which life insurance companies invest in debt and equity issues. This routing of savings through approximately 2,000 life insurance companies to the ultimate borrower makes the insurance companies financial intermediaries. The long-term and highly predictable nature of their insurance contract liabilities enables life insurance companies to require less liquidity and leads them to lock in yields over a longer period than the depository intermediaries. In 1988, life insurance companies held about 63% of their assets in the form of securities and 73% of these were corporate bonds. About 20% of their assets are in mortgages.

4.3.1.2 PROPERTY AND CASUALTY COMPANIES

Because the property and casualty companies receive premiums before the insured losses occur, they have a substantial amount of funds to invest and hence also act as an intermediary. Because the predictability of claims for property and casualty losses is less than that for life insurance claims, the property and casualty insurance companies typically hold more liquid assets than the life insurance companies but are still longer term investors than the depository intermediaries.

The two types of insurance companies combined invest about 15% of their assets in mortgage loans and 60% in stocks and bonds. They are a leading investor in corporate bonds. In 1987, they held $429 billion of their total assets of $1,394 billion (31%) in corporate bonds.

4.3.2 PENSION FUNDS

Pension funds collect contributions from individuals and employers in order to pay retirement benefits in subsequent years. Because the contributions precede benefit payouts, the pension funds invest the surplus and thus are financial intermediaries. In 1987 the pension funds held $1,559 in total assets that were largely invested in long-term debt and equities.

4.3.3 MUTUAL FUNDS

Mutual funds (once called investment companies) sell shares and invest the proceeds in a wide variety of assets. Those who purchase the shares (shareholders) like depositors in mutual savings banks, own the company and receive the net income. Unlike deposits, the shares have no fixed maturity date and must be sold in order for the shareholder to redeem his/her invested principal plus dividends. **Open-end** mutual funds repurchase the shares at the request of the shareholder and hence the total number of shares fluctuates as investors buy and sell open-end mutual fund shares. If the fund does not charge a fee for the purchase of its shares, it is a **no-load fund**; if a purchase fee is charged it is a **load fund**. **Closed-end** mutual funds issue a fixed number of shares at the formation of a fund and shareholders must sell their shares to other investors. Many such shares are traded on the New York Stock Exchange.

4.3.3.1 MONEY MARKET MUTUAL FUNDS

Mutual funds are classified by the nature of their investment strategies. One major distinction is between money market mutual funds and bond and equity funds. **Money market funds** restrict their investment to highly liquid money market instruments such as Treasury bills. The growth in these funds exploded between 1978 and 1982 due to the rapid rise in interest rates on money market instruments at a time when savings institutions were restrained from paying high rates by state and federal regulations. The partial deregulation of depository institutions has enabled these institutions to compete more effectively than before, but the money market funds have continued to attract a large volume of funds (over $260 billion in 1988). Due to the liquid nature of money market mutual funds, it is possible, but unlikely, that the sale of fund shares could result in a capital loss. The lack of insurance and the possibility of capital losses make these intermediary claims more risky than the claims of the above intermediaries.

4.3.3.2 BOND AND EQUITY MUTUAL FUNDS

Bond and equity mutual funds have the same characteristics as money market mutual funds except that these funds invest primarily in bonds and equities. The distribution of bond and equity mutual fund assets is given in Figure 4.1.

4.3.4 FINANCE COMPANIES

Finance companies raise funds by issuing their own equity or debt and use the funds to make relatively high risk, short-term loans. **Consumer Finance Companies**, such as Household Finance Corporation, make loans to individual consumers to finance purchases of consumer goods or to consolidate consumers' debts. **Sales Finance Companies**, such as General Motors Acceptance Corporation, make loans to consumers to purchase specific goods such as GM automobiles and trucks. **Business (or Commercial) Finance Companies** provide funds to businesses by purchasing the businesses' accounts receivables, enabling the businesses selling their accounts receivables to gain immediate access to funds. This is

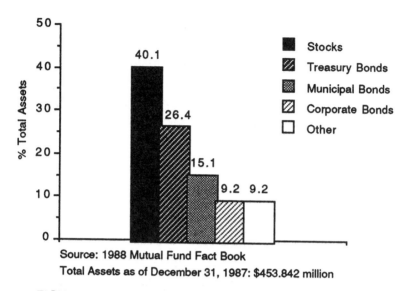

Source: 1988 Mutual Fund Fact Book
Total Assets as of December 31, 1987: $453.842 million

FIGURE 4.1–Bond and Equity Mutual Funds Assets

known as **factoring**. Some business finance companies purchase capital goods (like computers) and lease them to businesses.

Table 4.4 on the next page summarizes the preceding information about the major assets and liabilities of financial intermediaries.

4.4   REGULATION OF DEPOSITORY INSTITUTIONS

4.4.1 THE REGULATORY STRUCTURE

4.4.1.1 REGULATION OF COMMERCIAL BANKS

When banks are formed, they must either obtain a charter from the Comptroller of Currency or from a state agency. Banks chartered by the Comptroller of Currency are **national banks** and subject to federal regulations and annual unannounced examination by the comptroller's examiners. Banks

Table 4.4
Primary Portfolio Elements and Regulators of
Financial Intermediaries

Intermediary	Primary Assets	Primary Liabilities	Primary Regulators
Commercial Banks	Business and Other Loans	Deposits	Federal Reserve, FDIC State Commissions, othe
Savings and Loan Associations	Mortgage Loans	Deposits	FSLIC, Federal Home Loan Bank
Mutual Savings Banks	Mortgage Loans	Deposits	Federal Home Loan Ban State Commissions
Credit Unions	Consumer Loans	Deposits	Nat. Credit Union Admn.
Money Market Mutual Funds	Money Market Instruments	Shares	Securities and Exchang Commission
Bond and Equity Mutual Funds	Bonds and Equities	Shares	Securiites and Exchang Commission
Insurance Companies	Bonds and Equities	Insurance Policies	State Insurance Comm. Federal Agencies
Pension Funds	Equities, Bonds Mortgages	Pension Contracts	Federal Regulation
Finance Companies	Short-term Consumer Debt and Factoring	Equity and Long-term Debt	State Agencies

with state charters are **state banks** and are subject to the regulations of the state in which they are chartered. Further, state banks may and national banks must be members of the Federal Reserve System. Banks belonging to the Federal Reserve system are called **member banks**. Until 1980, the reserve requirements set by the FED were typically greater than state reserve requirements, and thus were a disincentive for banks to be member banks. Some stricter FED regulations still inhibit FED membership. Finally, all member banks must and state banks may join the **FDIC** (Federal Deposit Insurance Corporation). About 41% of all banks are member banks, 33% national banks, and over 96% are members of the FDIC.

The regulatory agencies recognized that their jurisdictions overlapped and have split the regulation of banks where they overlap by having the

FDIC regulate FDIC insured, nonmember, state banks;

Comptroller of Currency regulate national banks;

Federal Reserve System regulate state chartered, member banks and **bank holding companies** (corporations that own one or more banks).

The bank examinations are intended to

prevent fraud,

determine whether banks are in compliance with relevant regulations,

determine whether the banks are being appropriately managed.

The main areas of attention are denoted by **CAMEL** (capital adequacy, management, earnings and liquidity).

The FDIC was established to insure bank deposits and thereby prevent panics that produced **bank runs** (large numbers of deposit withdrawal attempts in a short time) that led to the failure of many banks in the 1930s. Currently, an individual's deposits in each bank are insured up to $100,000. Insured deposits account for about 75% of all bank deposits.

When a bank fails, the FDIC uses the **payoff method** or the **deposit assumption method**. In the first case, the FDIC pays depositors up to $100,000 from the funds gained by deposit insurance premiums and liquidates the assets of the bank. The proceeds from selling the bank's assets are used to pay creditors, including individuals whose deposits were in excess of $100,000. The assumption method involves arranging for a sound bank to merge with the failed bank and assume (accept) 100% of the failed bank's deposits. The merger is made attractive when the FDIC provides low cost loans to the sound bank and purchases some of the questionable assets of the failed bank. The rise in bank failures since 1972 has led many to conclude that FDIC premiums and reserves may not be sufficiently high and that bank capital levels are too low.

The FDIC is primarily concerned with regulation of banks to enhance the soundness of banks. The Federal Reserve and Comptroller of Currency also issue and enforce regulations designed to promote competitive banking markets and nondiscriminatory banking practices. The Antitrust Division of the U.S. Justice Department is also involved in enforcing federal laws concerned with anticompetitive bank actions. The Securities and Exchange Commission's sphere of influence includes bank issuance of securities and bank disclosure of information concerning the securities.

4.4.1.2 REGULATION OF OTHER FINANCIAL INTERMEDIARIES

As the last column of Table 4.4 suggests, the diverse nature of the nonbank intermediaries is matched by a diverse set of regulatory authorities. Of particular interest in the 1980s is the regulation of mutual savings banks and savings and loan associations as their failure rate has strained the abilities of the regulators. **The Federal Home Loan Bank System (FHLBS)** is the primary regulator of these thrifts, including both federal and state chartered members. The **FSLIC** (Federal Savings and Loan Insurance Corporation), a part of the FHLBS, provides deposit insurance for the customer's first $100,000 in deposits in a savings and loan or mutual savings bank. Maturity mismatches (see section 5.2.3) in periods of rising interest rates, weaknesses in oil and real estate markets, inability to compete with commercial banks, and, in some cases, fraudulent management contributed to dramatic failures in the thrift industry. Between 1980 and 1982 alone, the number of savings and loans and mutual savings banks decreased by 17% and 8%, respectively. The massive failure rates overtaxed the capacity of the FSLIC to find merger partners and the funds held by the FSLIC were inadequate to employ the payoff method in all cases so that many thrifts that should have been liquidated were allowed to continue operation. Congress is currently considering legislation to deal with this crisis.

4.4.2 DEREGULATION OF DEPOSITORY INSTITUTIONS IN THE 1980s

As indicated above, the rise in interest rates stimulated a disintermediation process that threatened the survival of many depository institutions. Further, the commercial banks increasingly complained about the Regulation Q provisions that enabled thrifts (mutual savings banks and savings and loans) to pay .5% more on savings deposits than banks could. The thrifts argued that their inability to issue checkable deposits and to make a wider variety of loans and investments put them at a competitive disadvantage relative to commercial banks.

The response to the problems of depository institutions was a two-stage legislative venture. The Depository Institutions Deregulation and Monetary Control Act of 1980 by the Congress enabled savings and loans to make consumer loans and to invest in commercial paper and corporate bonds as long as the total exposure to these assets was 20% or less. Mutual savings banks were permitted to make commercial loans as long as these assets were 5% or less of their total assets. It also provided that all depository institutions could issue NOW and

ATS accounts. **NOW** (negotiable orders of withdrawal) accounts are, in effect, interest bearing checking accounts. **ATS** (automatic transfer of savings) accounts allow for checkable deposit funds in excess of a certain amount to be automatically transferred to a savings account and for a reverse flow to take place when a check is drawn on an account with too low a balance. These innovations allow the depository institutions to compete with money market mutual funds. Further, the 1980 act required that Regulation Q, which set maximum interest rates on deposits, be phased out. It removed the **usury ceiling** (maximum interest rates that can be charged by lenders) on mortgages and provided for a three year suspension of usury ceilings on many business and agricultural loans (subject to possible reinstatement by states). In order to improve the FED's monetary control and to reduce the competitive advantage of nonmember banks, the act made all checkable deposits subject to a uniform set of reserve requirements set by the FED.

Despite these changes, the rate of failures of thrifts remained high and led to the **Depository Institutions Act of 1982 (Garn-St. Germain Act)**. It permitted depository institutions to offer **MMDA** (money market deposit accounts) that allowed the institutions to offer rates competitive with money market mutual funds and exempted the deposits from reserve requirements. These accounts permitted only three check and three preauthorized withdrawals per month. Subsequently, the committee administering the act approved **Super Now Accounts** that allow unlimited checks but carry a minimum deposit of $2,500. Also, the act further broadened the scope of lending by federally chartered thrifts by permitting them to carry 10% of their assets in commercial loans and 30% in consumer loans. Since the thrifts now were to have deposits and investments similar to those of commercial banks, the preferential treatment of the thrifts under Regulation Q was eliminated.

4.5 PROGRAMS AND INSTITUTIONS ENHANCING MORTGAGE LENDING

For nearly sixty years, the federal government has provided a wide variety of programs designed to promote home ownership. Through the **FHA** (Federal Housing Administration) and the **VA** (Veterans Administration), it seeks to reduce the risk of mortgage loans by providing federal insurance against borrower defaults. As mentioned above, mismatches of maturities of mortgage loans and deposit liabilities created problems for mortgage lenders. To address these problems, three agencies were created between 1937 and 1970:

FNMA (Federal National Mortgage Association, a.k.a. Fannie Mae), formed in 1937 as a federal agency and converted to a private corporation in 1966, serves to create a secondary market in federally insured mortgages. Using its association with the federal government to issue its own debt at favorable rates, FNMA raises funds and uses the proceeds to buy mortgage loans from thrifts and either holds the mortgages on its own account or resells them to other investors. By being ready to buy and sell the mortgages, FNMA provides liquidity to these loans.

GNMA (Government National Mortgage Association, a.k.a. Ginnie Mae), formed in 1968, also purchases mortgage loans (federally insured and conventional mortgages), but differs in that GNMA may subsidize the loan originator. If a lender makes a mortgage loan at a 10% rate and then finds that rates rise to 11% so that the market value of the 10% loan has fallen, GNMA can buy the mortgage at its face value rather than at the discounted market value, which provides a direct subsidy to – and makes mortgage loans more liquid for – the mortgage originator. GNMA can then sell the mortgage loan at its market value with the difference between the GNMA purchase and sales price being paid for by federal tax dollars. This reduces the market risk on mortgage loans issued by thrifts.

FHMLC (Federal Home Loan Mortgage Corporation, a.k.a. Freddie Mac), formed in 1970, was created to increase the marketability of conventional mortgages and to enable the Federal Home Loan Bank System to raise funds to provide loans to thrifts. FHMLC issues its own debt at rates lower than mortgage rates and uses the funds to buy mortgage loans from the mortgage originators which provides liquidity for savings and loans.

CHAPTER 5

COMMERCIAL BANK MANAGEMENT

In the prior chapter, the commercial banks were characterized with rather broad descriptions. An examination of many individual banks and bank holding companies would reveal that they are very complex organizations. In economic jargon, the typical average to large scale bank would be considered an oligopolistic, multiproduct (or multiservice) firm operating in input and output markets characterized by uncertainty and short- and long-term volatility of assets and liabilities. Consider the elements individually:

Oligopolistic – this indicates that the banks operate in markets where their strategies take into account the tactics of rival banks and that banks believe that their average revenue (demand) curves for loans are downward sloping.

Multiproduct – the banks provide many various products (detailed below).

Uncertainty of inputs and outputs – the banks operate in markets in which the prices of inputs, such as borrowed funds, and prices of outputs, such as rates charged on business loans, cannot be perfectly predicted.

Volatility of assets and liabilities – the volume of assets, such as loans, and liabilities, such as demand deposits, are subject to variation in both the short run and the long run.

5.1   OVERVIEW OF BANK ACTIVITIES

While it is correct to say that banks primarily raise funds by raising deposits at one set of interest rates and invest the proceeds in loans and certain securities at another set of interest rates, it is important to realize that these deposits and investments are of a wide variety. Furthermore, through the use of bank holding companies, the actual sphere of bank activities is much larger. A **bank holding company** is a corporation that owns or controls one or more banks. Bank holding companies were formed in order to avoid the restrictions on business activities permitted by commercial banks – charter restrictions and regulatory rules. Table 5.1 lists activities approved for bank holding companies by the FED.

Table 5.1
NonBank Activities Approved
for Bank Holding Companies

Dealer in Bankers' Acceptances
Mortgage Banking
Consulting on Employee Benefits
Factoring
Industrial Banking
Investment Advising
Tax Planning and Preparation
Data Processing
Acquisition of Failing Thrifts in Other States
Commodity Trading Advisory Service
Tax Planning and Preparation

Authorization Services on Credit Cards
Reporting Services for Lost or Stolen Credit Cards
Land Escrow Service
Futures Commission Merchant
Sales of Information, Advice, and Transactions in Foreign
    Exchange
Insurance Agent or Broker Credit Servicing
Underwriting Credit Life and Credit Accident and Health
    Insurance
Servicing Student Loans
Finance Companies
Credit Card Issuing
Trust Company
Full-Payout Leasing
Sales of Economic Information
Bookkeeping
Real Estate Appraisals
Armored Car Services
Consumer Financial Consulting
Credit Agency or Bureau
Sales of Travelers' Checks
Bullion Broker
Sale of Money Orders
Discount Brokerage Services
Courier Service
Management Consulting to Other Banks and Thrifts

Many bank holding companies hold only one bank so that
the distinction between the activities of the bank holding company and the bank are merely legal distinctions and the bank is
best thought of as a multiproduct firm with a wide array of
activities. For the rest of this chapter, however, the traditional
financial services of banks will be emphasized.

5.1.1 ASSETS AND LIABILITES OF COMMERCIAL BANKS

Panels B and D of Table 5.2 summarize the assets and liabilities of commercial banks.

Table 5.2
Income, Expenses and Portfolio of
Commercial Banks, 1987

Panel A–Income and Expenses

Operating Income: Total	$281,215	%
Interest-Total	236,531	84.11
Loans	173,160	61.6
Balances with banks	11,872	4.222
Fed Funds Sold	8,808	3.132
Securities	42,691	15.18
Service Charges on Deposits	8,655	3.078
Other Income	36,029	12.81

Panel B–Portfolio Composition %Assets

Interest Earning Assets		86.62%
Loans		
Commercial–Industrial	20.05	
Real Estate	18.68	58.36
Consumer	11.1	
Securities		
U.S. Government	10.04	
State & Local Gov.	6.25	18.57
Other	2.28	
Gross Fed Funds Sold		4.43
Interest-bearing Deposits		5.26
Other Assets		13.38%

Panel C–Operating Expenses:

Total:	$274,060	%
Interest: Total	142,325	51.9
Deposits	113,634	41.6
Large CD	18,919	6.903
Deposits in Foreign Offices	25,945	9.467
Other Deposits	68,770	25.09
Fed Funds Purchased	15,740	5.743
Other Borrowing	12,950	4.725
Salaries & Benefits	44,528	16.25
Occupancy Expense	15,301	5.583
Loss Provision	36,337	13.26
Other Expenses	35,569	12.98
Securites gains/losses	1,394	0.509
Net Income after Taxes	3,429	1.251

Panel D–Liabilities and Capital

		%	
Deposit Liabilities			76.42
Foreign Offices		11.38	
Domestic Offices		65.04	
Demand	15.4		
Other Checkable	6.01		
Large Time	10.6		
Other Deposits	33.02		
Gross Fed Funds Purchased			8.06
Other Borrowing			4.45
Other and Capital			11.0

The data clearly indicate that the primary type of investment by commercial banks is in loans to businesses and consumers, and that the main sources of funds are the checkable and time deposits. If the types of loans made were compared to thrifts, the notable distinction would be the greater diversification of bank loans. However, there are a number of **restrictions on bank loans and investments** which include the following:

National banks cannot loan more than 15% of their equity to one agent.

National banks can make only limited loans to directors and officers.

Investments in stocks are generally prohibited, except for trust activities.

Bank holding company loans to affiliates must meet a range of regulations.

Loans made to purchase stocks are subject to FED margin requirements.

5.1.2 REVENUES AND COSTS OF COMMERCIAL BANKS

Panels A and C of Table 5.2 illustrate the nature of the primary sources of income and costs for commercial banks. Not surprisingly, the pattern of income reflects the distribution of assets. With the majority of assets in various kinds of loans, it follows that the primary sources of revenue are interest and fees earned on loans.

The **costs incurred by banks** are derived from two major sources:

(1) Costs incurred in attracting funds to the bank:

Interest and promotional expenses associated with inducing persons to deposit funds in the bank.

Costs of borrowing funds, such as interest on federal funds.

(2) Costs incurred in operations and services:

Costs of providing deposit services.

Management of customer investments.

Management of the bank's own investments and loans.

Other.

5.1.3 BANK MARKET STRUCTURES

Because of legal restrictions on branch banking, interstate banking, and multiple bank offices within certain areas, there are a large number of small banks in the U.S. Smaller banks (those with $25 million or less in assets), accounting for about 38% of the 15,000 banks in the U.S., held only 3.2% of total assets of insured banks. The hundred largest banks held about 45% of total bank assets. Among most countries, there are typically only a handful of banks within the country but there are typically a large number of bank branches. In the U.S., about 7,000 of the banks are branch banks with nearly 47,000 branches. The total number of banking offices of various sorts is in excess of 61,000. Chart 5.1 indicates that the tendency during the past 40 years has been for the number of banks to decline while the number of branches increases.

Market structures refers to the kind of competition in the industry. In highly competitive market structures, the firm is such a small part of the industry that it acts as a price taker for both inputs (such as deposits) and outputs (such as loans). **Price takers** are economic agents that believe that they cannot charge output prices higher than the prevailing market price and cannot buy inputs at prices below the prevailing input prices. The bank numbers above would appear to suggest that the banking industry has little concentration of economic power, and hence, is nearly perfectly competitive. However, they do not imply that the small banks are highly competitive; on the contrary, in many cases there are only one or two banks

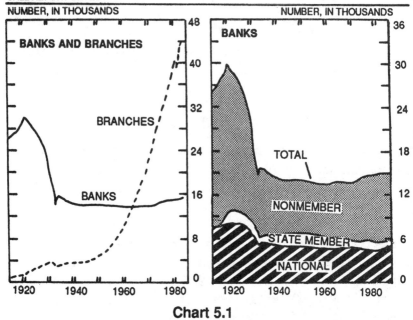

Chart 5.1

in a small town so that the banks have substantial market power within that area. Larger banks, which gather deposits and make loans to firms across the whole or a large part of the country, face a large degree of competition, and hence, are not able to set the rates paid on deposits and on loans. On the other hand, in small and moderate sized communities where the banks are relatively small, there may be one or a few small banks so that these behave as oligopolistic firms with some degree of price making capacity. The market structure affects the nature of the demand curve facing a bank. For highly competitive markets, the demand curve will be highly elastic (very flat) such as $D_{competitive}$ in Figure 5.1; if the market is perfectly competitive, the firm's demand (average revenue) curve will be horizontal. For markets in which there are few firms, however, the demand curve will be less elastic (steeper) like $D_{oligopoly}$. If a single bank is the only source of loanable funds, the demand curve for loans in that market is the same as that bank's loan

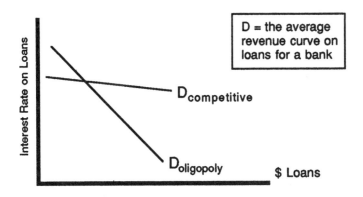

FIGURE 5.1–Examples of Loan Demand Curves for Various Market Structures

demand curve. A similar kind of analysis holds for the supply of deposits to the bank. In highly competitive markets, the bank will have very little opportunity to pay interest rates below the rate charged by other banks in its market.

5.2 BANK ASSET AND LIABILITY MANAGEMENT

Banks presumably maximize profits as do other private sector firms. To do so, the bank seeks to find the portfolio of assets and liabilities that provides the largest difference between revenues and costs, given the constraints faced by the bank. The inputs of the firm are the labor and physical capital, such as computers, coin counters, etc., similar to those inputs of many nonbank firms. The bank, however, differs in that it must compete for deposit liabilities and other sources of funds and then invest those funds in loans, bonds, and other financial instruments while satisfying constraints that are of a nature peculiar to the banking industry.

66

5.2.1 CONSTRAINTS FACED BY BANK MANAGERS

The commercial bank attempts to maximize profits subject to constraints imposed by the following:

requirements concerning the bank capital,

reserve requirements set by the FED,

the need to maintain liquidity,

and limitations on types of loans and investments (see section 5.1.1).

The regulations established by the FED and other regulators and the uncertainty about loan requests and deposit flows that produce a need for liquidity constrain the bank's portfolio choices. These restrictions are discussed below, and then the profit maximizing portfolio choices are illustrated.

5.2.1.1 BANK CAPITAL REQUIREMENTS

Bank capital consists of **primary capital**, equity obtained by the issue of stocks plus retained profits, and **secondary capital**, subordinated notes and debentures. Subordinated debt, in this case, means that the other creditors' claims (e.g., depositors) will be satisfied first in the event of failure of the bank. Bank capital is both a source of funds for the bank to invest in earning assets and a safety cushion against bank failure. If a bank with $100 million in assets and $5 million in capital suffers a 10% drop in the value of its assets due to declines in security prices, fraud, or defaults, the bank would be insolvent. If it had $12 million in capital, it would survive the drop in asset values. Federal Reserve, FDIC, and Comptroller of Currency regulators require banks to maintain a minimum capital-to-asset ratio of 5.5%, and in the case of riskier loans and investments, their guidelines require much higher ratios. State capital requirements are generally less demanding.

While higher capital-to-asset ratios provide a better safety cushion, bankers do not view them as unambiguously desireable because low capital-to-asset ratios provide high leverage for invested funds. For example, a bank with $100,000 in net worth with $10,000 in profits earned on $1,000,000 in assets would have a rate of return of 1% on assets ($10,000 ÷ $1,000,000) and a 10% return on net worth ($10,000 ÷ $100,000). A more highly leveraged bank with the same amount of assets and income, but having $50,000 in net worth, would have a 1% return on assets, but a 20% return on net worth ($10,000 ÷ $50,000). An investor in the first bank would earn $1 for each $10 invested while an investor in the second bank would earn $2 for each $10 invested. The advantages of leveraging lead some banks to desire a lower capital ratio than that mandated by its regulators, and hence, the capital requirements restrict the bank's portfolio choices.

5.2.1.2 BANK RESERVE REQUIREMENTS

All financial institutions that offer deposits must meet the reserve requirements set by the Federal Reserve Board. The banks must have either currency in their vaults or funds being held by a district federal reserve bank. For most banks, each additional dollar of checkable deposits requires an additional $.12 in reserves to satisfy the FED regulation. If a bank wishes to raise funds by attracting deposits subject to reserve requirements, it must raise more funds than it will invest. For example, if the bank wants to invest $100,000 in a bond, it must raise more than $100,000 in demand deposits. With a 12% reserve ratio, it must attract $113,636.36 in demand deposits so that after spending $100,000 on the bond, the bank will have $13,636.64 additional reserves to meet the additional reserve requirements due to the new deposits. In general, if the bank is to invest an additional ΔB in bonds and the reserves ratio is r, the additional demand deposits it must attract, ΔD, can be calculated as: $\Delta D = [\Delta B \div (1 - r)]$. The reserve requirements thus restrict the portfolio choices of the bank by forcing the bank to hold reserves; the greater the reserve ratio, the more reserves that must be held. Reserve requirements not only restrict the bank's allocation of resources; they raise the effective cost of invested funds.

5.2.1.3 LIQUIDITY NEEDS

In order to provide liquidity, banks hold primary reserves and secondary reserves. **Primary reserves** consist of the following:

>vault cash,

>funds on deposit at the Federal Reserve Banks,

>commercial banks' deposits at other commercial banks.

Many smaller banks deposit their own funds in larger commercial banks as a part of a **correspondent bank** relationship. The larger bank may, for example, sort checks or buy and sell securities for the smaller bank and use the smaller bank's deposits to carry out the transactions.

Secondary reserves are bank holdings of liquid securities, such as Treasury bills, that may be readily sold with little market risk. In addition to holding reserves to satisfy FED requirements, banks also hold secondary reserves because of the uncertainty of cash flows into the bank and due to uncertainty about the demand for loans. Even if the bank had no reserve requirements, it would need to hold some reserves in order to clear checks and to meet customer demands for currency. A bank may hold excess reserves in case of unexpectedly large flows of deposits out of the bank, or it may hold other liquid assets such as Treasury bills. Similarly, to meet customer demands for currency, the bank must carry some vault cash and make arrangements through sales of assets or borrowing to quickly raise currency in the event of unexpectedly large customer requests for currency.

If, for example, a bank currently has required reserves of $10 million and suffers an unexpected increase in checks being cleared against the bank in the amount of $1 million, it will have to absorb the reserve loss by:

holding fewer excess reserves,

selling an asset such as Treasury bills.

Because the longer-term bonds have a greater market risk, banks will frequently desire to hold a liquid, money market asset in order to raise funds in the event of greater reserve needs. Some banks provide for the needed liquidity by holding excess reserves; such holdings are minimal since they do not bear an interest income. Banks with access to the large denomination CD market or brokered CD funds, may provide for the reserve need by issuing CDs. While banks do compete for funds through savings, time, and consumer CDs, the amounts of these funds raised are not readily manipulated on a day-to-day basis.

5.2.2 UNCONSTRAINED PROFIT MAXIMIZATION PORTFOLIOS

If banks were not uncertain about customer needs, deposit flows, defaults, and future interest rates, and had zero reserve requirements, the profit maximization problem of the bank would be simple. In this case the bank would invest until the marginal revenues of all assets were equal to the marginal cost of all sources of funds. For example, if the bank could invest only in automobile loans, A_{loans}, and business loans, B_{loans}, and could raise funds only from demand deposits, D, and time deposits T, the profit-maximizing conditions for the bank would be:

$$MR_{Aloans} = MR_{Bloans} = MR_{bank}$$

$$MC_D = MC_T = MC_{bank}$$

$$MR_{bank} = MC_{bank}$$

Figure 5.2 illustrates the profit maximizing situation for this case. The example shows that when marginal costs and revenues are both $.1, the asset and liability combinations produce the highest profit the bank can earn. The marginal costs include any interest paid plus other costs, such as printing costs.

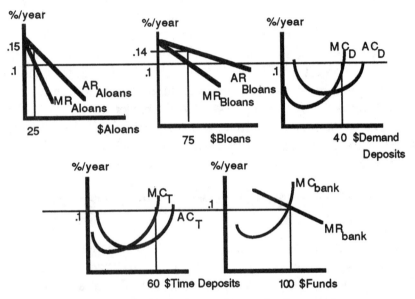

AR = average revenue, firm's demand curve for the asset
AC = average total cost of raising funds from the liability

FIGURE 5.2–Example of Triple Profit Maximization Condition

In this example, the bank has raised funds from each source until the marginal cost of each is .1% and has invested in each asset until the marginal revenues are equal to .1. Although the marginal revenues from each asset are equal, the rates charged the customer are not equal for the two assets. In this example, the rate on A_{loans} is 15% and the rate on B_{loans} is 14%.

To understand that the triple equality does imply the optimum portfolio, suppose that it did not hold and consider the profit opportunities. For example, suppose MR_{Bloan} = 15% and MR_{Aloan} = 10%; in this case, switching a dollar of funds from loans to bonds would yield an increase in profit of $.05. If the equality of MRs does not hold, profits can be increased by pulling funds from the low MR and reinvesting in the high MR asset until there is no gain from the switch, which means all marginal revenues would be equal.

Similarly, suppose the marginal costs are not equal; we can show that the cost of funds can be reduced by switching funds from the high to low marginal cost funds. For example, if MC_D = 10% and MC_T = 11%, reducing reliance on time deposits by $1 and expanding demand deposits by $1 would cause the cost of funds to fall by $.10. If such a change in liabilities can reduce costs, the mix cannot be the profit maximizing combination.

What if $MC_D = MC_T = MC_{bank}$, 10%, $MR_B = MR_L = MR_{bank}$ = 13%, so that $MR_{bank} > MC_{bank}$? Clearly, if additional funds are raised at a cost of less than 13% and invested at 13%, profits must increase. When $MR_{bank} > MC_{bank}$, the bank can expand both liabilities and assets and increase profits. If $MR_{bank} = MC_{bank}$, expanding liabilities and investing the funds would result in MC increasing and MR declining so that each extra dollar raised and invested would return less than it cost to raise.

5.2.3 EFFECTS OF RISKS ON BANK PORTFOLIOS

When the various uncertainties the banks actually face are considered, the optimal portfolio will usually differ from that suggested by the above conditions. The bank must, of course, meet its mandated capital requirements and reserve requirements set by the FED. In addition, the portfolio chosen by banks will reflect the desire to reduce the following:

Risk of Insolvency

Interest Rate Risk

Default Risk

Poor Customer Relations

Mismatches of Maturities of Assets and Liabilities

If the bank is sufficiently risk averse, it may keep the amount of capital above the mandated minimum in order to reduce the possibility of insolvency in the event of loan defaults or declines in the market prices of assets when interest rates rise.

Further, given the volatility of deposits and customer loan demands, the bank may wish to carry some excess reserves and will usually hold some money market instruments that it can sell with little market risk if additional reserves are needed. It may be the case that the expected marginal revenue of 20 year bonds exceeds the expected marginal revenue of 90-day Treasury bills so that on purely immediate profit maximization grounds, the bank would hold only the bonds. But in view of the lower market risk of the Treasury bills, the bank will typically carry enough bills to hedge against possible capital losses if assets were to be sold to raise reserves.

Similarly, the possible marginal revenue on consumer loans may exceed that of loans to support business inventories, but if the consumer loans have a sufficiently high default risk, the bank will not invest heavily in consumer loans and make minimal business loans. Rather, the bank will consider the risk adjusted returns on various assets in making its portfolio choices and make more business loans and fewer of the risky consumer loans.

The need to maintain good customer relations is also an

important factor in bank portfolio decisions. Since the long run loan demand and sources of deposits to the bank depend on keeping bank customers satisfied, banks are not likely to deny a good customer a loan or to charge an exorbitant rate in order to maximize short run profits. A bank might be able to earn 18% on a 1 week federal funds loan while the rate earned on a loan to a long-term customer might be only 13%, and rather than antagonizing the customer, the bank may satisfy all or a part of the customer's loan request in order to maximize long run profits.

In order to reduce default risks, banks may not meet all of a customer's loan request. When banks do not provide all of the funds requested by a loan customer at the prevailing interest rate nor raise the rate to compensate for the risk, but provide a portion of the funds, the bank is engaged in **credit rationing**.

Another non-price means of dealing with customer requests is the practice of requiring compensating balances. In addition to the rate charged on loans or fees charged for services such as providing computer services, the bank may require **compensating balances**. For example, a bank may loan a firm $1 million at 5% and require that the firm keep $100,000 on deposit. Thus, the firm pays $50,000 for the use of $900,000 rather than $1 million which makes the effective cost of funds 5.55% (50,000/900,000). The firm may prefer this arrangement to borrowing $900,000 at 5.55% because it enables the firm to show $50,000 in cash on its balance sheet.

Another type of risk that the simple profit maximizing formulation ignored is **mismatches of maturities of assets and liabilities risk**. Consider the case of a bank that makes a one year loan at 8%, raising the funds by issuing a 90-day CD at 7%. If the rates on CDs rise 90 days later, the bank may find its cost of funds exceeding the return on the loan. Similarly, if the bank raises $1 million in 6 month CDs at 5% and invests the funds in 90 day Treasury bills at 5.5%, it faces the risk that after 90 days the rate on assets like Treasury bills will fall below 5%, producing a loss on each dollar invested. To avoid such risks, banks will consider matching the terms to maturity of assets with the terms to maturity of liabilities. A bank may make a 90 day loan today, at a rate based on the rate it pays by issuing a 90 day CD today, for example. In fact, many loans have floating rates in which the rate charged by the bank rises or falls as the 90-day CD or similar rate rises or falls so that the bank locks in a gross profit spread. Adjustable rate mortgages are also a reflection of the desire of banks to avoid maturity mismatches.

A recent innovation in banking that provides greater liquidity for the loan portfolio is the **securitization of loans**. This process bundles a large number of loans and sells the collection as if it were a security with guarantees made about the bundle rather than the individual loans. This eliminates the problem of selling individual loans in small denominations. Such small denomination loans require buyers to evaluate the default risk of many individual loans and make the loans illiquid (nonliquid) and unsalable at higher prices. A similar recent innovation is the bank issued **loan-backed security**. In this case the bank sells a security for which loans made to its customers are the collateral for the security. Unlike deposits issued by the bank, the loan-backed securities do not involve reserve requirements or FDIC insurance.

In sum, although a bank portfolio that equates the expected marginal revenue and marginal cost would provide the highest expected profit, such a portfolio ignores a variety of risks that a risk averse bank would not ignore.

5.2.4 HISTORICAL DEVELOPMENT OF THEORIES OF LIQUIDITY MANAGEMENT

The preceding analysis considered the problem of a bank in meeting its liquidity needs and maximizing profits in terms of contemporary economic theory. The literature on bank management provides several earlier perspectives that the student should be aware of:

The Commercial Loan or Real Bills Doctrine

The Shiftability Doctrine

The Anticipated Income Doctrine.

Liability Management

The **Commercial Loan Doctrine**, which was a common perspective during the first two decades of the Federal Reserve System's evolution, held that banks should make only commercial loans (loans to businesses) that were short-term, self-liquidating loans. The ideal loan, according to this doctrine, was one made to a firm to purchase raw materials to be transformed into finished goods for sale. Because it was presumed that the sale of the finished goods would provide the revenue to repay the loan, the loan was considered self-liquidating. Loans to purchase personal consumption items were not considered appropriate.

The commercial loan doctrine not only was thought to provide a rationale for sound banking practices, but its application was also thought to provide the increases and decreases in credit and money appropriate to finance economic expansions. There are several problems with this proposition about how banks should base their portfolios. First, it will not generally maximize profits at any given risk level. The demand for other types of loans by potential clients with solid credit standing is high enough to make those loans as attractive, or more so, than many commercial loans. Second, no loan is guaranteed to be self-liquidating. Even a loan for temporary inventories of resources will not be self-liquidating if the demand for the finished good is inadequate. Finally, as will be shown in Chapter 10, there is no reason to believe that the quantity of money and credit generated by banks providing commercial loans on demand would provide the correct amounts to provide for high employment and low inflation.

Most banks found in the 1930s that portfolios dominated by commercial and other loans did not provide the liquidity needed when banks experienced losses of reserves. This led to the wide-spread acceptance of the **Shiftability Thesis**, which held that bank liquidity could be guaranteed by bank purchases of "shiftable assets". Shiftable assets are assets that banks could readily "shift" to other investors. In modern terminology, shiftable assets are liquid assets such as 90-day Treasury bills. It does, in fact, make sense to maintain a portfolio of these secondary reserves or liquid assets that can be readily sold with low risk of capital loss when the bank needs additional reserves. However, it does not follow that the adoption of this by all banks guarantees that all banks can gain reserves by selling liquid assets. For example, suppose the economy was at a business cycle peak and that the demands for money and credit were so high that all banks in the system held zero excess reserves. Now suppose New Ross National Bank sells $10,000 in Treasury bills to Acme Inc. in order to gain reserves to support new deposits. When Acme Inc.'s check drawn against Chicago Trust Bank clears, Chicago Trust Bank will lose $10,000 in reserves and New Ross National Bank will gain reserves but there will be no new reserves for the banking system as a whole. If Chicago Trust Bank attempts to restore its reserves by selling its "shiftable assets", it will merely cause some other bank(s) to lose reserves. As long as the liquid assets are sold to private banks or other private agents, the sales will not provide new reserves to the banking system.

The **anticipated income doctrine** focused not on the type of assets held by the bank in meeting the liquidity needs of the bank, but on the flow of income from the assets. Proponents of this doctrine held that it did not matter whether the bank invested in commercial loans, home mortgages, or government bonds, as long as the revenue from the assets provided the desired amount of reserves. Hence, according to this theory, the banks should project their reserve needs into the future and then determine whether the anticipated income from the assets provided the reserve needed. While there is merit to the notion that the bank should take into account expected income, this view ignores the basic fact of life for bankers. That is, deposit flows and loan demands are not easily forecasted. The reason banks face liquidity problems is because of the uncertainty and volatility of these elements. Thus, it makes little sense to say that the bank can deal with the problem of uncertainty by anticipating the amounts of reserves.

During the early 1960s, banks began to focus on the liabilities side of the portfolio as a means of providing liquidity. When several large New York commercial banks began to act as dealers in the large denomination CDs, the potential for flexible management of liabilities existed. The existence of an active secondary market in CDs made these investments much more attractive to nonfinancial firms. Ford Motor Co., for example, would be more willing to put $5 million in a 90-day negotiable CD at Chase Manhattan Bank when the secondary market exists because it would be able to sell the CD at any time and, hence, was not locked into an investment for 90 days.

By varying the rates paid and other terms, the following liabilities can be used by banks in order to gain reserves to finance loans and investments:

Checkable Deposits

Small Time and Savings Deposits

Large Denomination Negotiable CDs*

Federal Funds*

Repurchase Agreements*

Borrowing from the Federal Reserve System#

Sales of Short-term Notes (by the bank holding company)*

Eurodollar Deposits*

Sales of Equity

The need for bank liquidity in order to deal with the volatility of reserves and loan requests has long been recognized. The commercial loan or real bills doctrine held that banks should meet the problem by making the correct type of loan. The shiftability doctrine changed the focus to the nature of the investments portfolio and held that it should contain "shiftable assets". The anticipated income doctrine emphasized the flow of expected income rather than the type of asset held. During the 1960s, banks began to aggressively market liabilities, especially negotiable CDs, in order to meet reserve needs. Modern bank management recognizes the risks and priorities in both asset and liability management.

---

* indicates that this item can be used relatively flexibly in the short run

a very temporary source of funds; see Chapter 7.

CHAPTER 6

THE MECHANICS OF MONEY
SUPPLY CREATION

In this chapter the process by which the money supply is generated is explained. It is widely but incorrectly believed that the federal government creates the money supply in the U.S. This chapter will show that the money supply is the joint product of the actions of the (1) nonbank public as it seeks to allocate its wealth and borrow funds, (2) the banks as they seek to maximize profits, and (3) the actions of the Federal Reserve System.

6.1 MULTIPLE EXPANSION OF DEPOSITS: THE ELEMENTS

6.1.1 RESERVE RATIOS AND RESERVE MEASURES

Central to the story of money supply creation is the **multiple expansion of deposits process** whereby new funds entering the banking system result in an increase of checkable deposits that are a multiple of the initial increase in funds injected into the banking system. A key element in the expansion process is the reserve ratio set by the Federal Reserve, FED. The FED requires that all depository institutions (commercial banks, savings and loans, mutual savings banks, and credit unions) maintain a minimum amount of reserves for each dollar of certain deposits. This minimum ratio of reserves to deposits, called the **reserve ratio**, is associated with the upper limit for the multiple expansion of deposits. The exact reserve requirements are given in Chapter 7; for illustration assume that the FED requires banks (banks are taken to represent all depository institutions) to keep $.10 in reserves for each dollar of deposits. The reserves may be held in the vault of the bank or at the FED. The actual amount of reserves is known as **total reserves**, RT. The amount of reserves that the bank is obligated to hold by FED regulations is called **required reserves**, RR, and the difference between total and required reserves is **excess reserves**, RE.

6.1.2 ILLUSTRATION OF THE DEPOSIT EXPANSION PROCESS USING BANK BALANCE SHEETS

We now outline how the combination of this reserve requirement and banks' profit seeking will lead to a money creation process involving a multiple expansion of deposits when new funds are injected into the banking system. For the following illustration, assume that the money supply, M, is the sum of currency, C, and checkable deposits, D. For simplicity, it is assumed that people do not want to convert any of their new deposits into currency and that banks, which start with zero excess reserves, do not wish to add any excess reserves.

Suppose a customer deposits $1000 in currency at Bank America. Using the incremental T-account, we show the net change in Bank America's balance sheet as:

Bank America

Assets		Liabilities + Net Worth	
Reserves	+1000	Deposits	+ 1000

The incremental T-account shows the net, cumulative effects of transactions on bank assets and liabilities.

Since deposits, D, have risen by $1000 ($\Delta D = 1000$) and the reserve ratio is 10%, the required reserves, RR, of the bank are now $100 higher than before [$\Delta RR = .1(\Delta D)$]. But since total reserves, RT, have risen by $1000, the bank's excess reserves, RE have risen by $900 [$\Delta RE = \Delta RT - \Delta RR = 1000 - .1(1000) = 900$]. At this point the money supply has not changed since the rise in deposits is exactly offset by the decline in currency. [$\Delta M = \Delta C + \Delta D = -\$1000 + \$1000 = \$0$]

Bank America now has $900 in excess reserves that do not generate revenue and hence will typically seek to loan these funds to a customer, say Acme Corp, in order to earn interest. When it does so, its incremental T-account will appear as:

Bank America

Assets		Liabilities + Net Worth	
Reserves	+1000	Deposits	+ 1900
Loans	+ 900		

The Acme Corp would not borrow the funds and let them sit idle for long while paying interest, rather, it would spend the funds. Suppose Acme buys fuel oil from Petro Inc for $900. When Petro Inc deposits Acme's check in Bronx Bank, Bronx Bank will send the check to the FED to collect the funds from

Bank America. When Bank America certifies to the FED that it is indeed a bona fide check for which Acme has funds on deposit, the FED will transfer $900 from Bank America's reserve account to that of Bronx Bank. Bank America's incremental T-account will appear as:

Bank America

Assets		Liabilities + Net Worth	
Reserves	+100	Deposits	+ 1000
Loans	+900		

At this point Bank America's actual reserves and required reserves are up by $100 and hence the bank now has zero excess reserves. If Bank America had made a loan in an amount greater than its excess reserves, when the loan customer wrote checks in the amount of the loan and the checks were cleared by the FED, Bank America would have negative excess reserves; that is, it would not have sufficient reserves to meet FED requirements and would be subject to penalties imposed by the FED. Hence, the **rule of thumb is that a single bank in a multiple bank system can "safely" lend out only the amount of its excess reserves.**

Note that the money supply has now risen by $900 since $[\Delta M = \Delta C + \Delta D = -\$1000 + \$1900]$. Bronx Bank's incremental T-account is:

Bronx Bank

Assets		Liabilities + Net Worth	
Reserves	+900	Deposits	+900

Now Bronx has additional total reserves of $900, additional required reserves of $90 $[\Delta RR = .1(900)]$ and additional excess reserves of $810 ($\Delta RE = 900 - 90$) and can safely lend out $810. When Bronx Bank does lend $810 to a customer, say Widget Co., who buys $ 810 in services from CompuStix with an account in Carthage National Bank, and all checks have cleared, the incremental T-accounts for Bronx Bank and Carthage National Bank will be:

Bronx Bank

Assets		Liabilities + Net Worth	
Reserves	+90	Deposits	+900
Loans	+810		

Carthage National Bank

Assets		Liabilites + Net Worth	
Reserves	+810	Deposits	+810

Deposits have now risen by a total of $2,710. The process thus is creating larger and larger amounts of deposits. If banks keep lending out the excess reserves and customers do not withdraw currency from the banks, it can be shown that eventually deposits will rise by $10,000, or in general the deposits will rise by [ΔRT/reserve ratio], which in this case is [(1000/.1) = 10,000]. The expansion process is summarized in Table 6.1.

The following example assumes that banks want exactly zero excess reserves, that no currency withdrawals occurred, and that there is only one type of deposit subject to reserve requirements. While these assumptions are not strictly accurate, the above illustrates the nature of the process of loan and deposit expansion. It also illustrates that an injection of funds into the banking system results in a multiplier effect; that is, the net change in the money supply is a multiple of the change in funds available to support deposits. The deposit multiplier in

Table 6.1
Deposit Expansion Process for a Required
Reserve Ratio of .1

Bank	New Deposit	Cumulative System Deposit	For the Current Bank		
			ΔRT	ΔRR	ΔRE
America	$1000	$1000	$1000	$100	$900
Bronx	900	1900	900	90	810
Carthage	810	2710	810	81	729
Danville	729	3439	729	72.9	656.1
•	•	•	•	•	•
•	•	•	•	•	•
•	•	•	•	•	•
Final System Total:	$10,000	$10,000	$1000	$100	$0

the example was 10. With the current assumptions the formula for the deposit multiplier is:

$$D = RT \div r \text{ and } \Delta D = \Delta D \div r.$$

where RT is the total amount of reserves in the banking system, D is the amount of total deposits, r is the required reserve ratio, and the Δ indicates the change in the value. A similar and equally tedious expansion process for M1 and M2 can be shown by T-accounts, but a more satisfactory method for relating monetary expansion to the actual and potential reserves of the banking system is available through the monetary base multiplier framework.

6.2 DERIVATION OF BASE MULTIPLIERS FOR M1 AND M2

6.2.1 INTRODUCTION TO THE MONETARY BASE AND BASE MULTIPLIER CONCEPTS

When the banks and the public have fully adjusted their portfolios, the deposit expansion process described above results in the money supply being proportional to the monetary base. The **monetary base or high-powered money** is the sum of the currency held by the nonbank public (including firms) and the reserves held by depository institutions in the form of vault cash, or funds deposited by the institutions at the Federal Reserve. The money supply is related to the base as follows:

$$M = kB$$

k = base multiplier; a number such as 2.4
B = monetary base; a number such as $300 billion

The monetary base is the sum of currency held by the public, C, and the total reserves, RT, of the banking system. The base multiplier reflects the portfolio choices by banks and the public and the reserve ratios established by the FED. The base multiplier for the M1 measure of the money supply is derived as follows:

6.2.2 KEY BANK AND PUBLIC PORTFOLIO RATIOS

Let:

c be the public's currency (C) to checkable deposit (D) ratio; $c = C/D$; e.g. $c = .1$ means that the public wants to carry $1 in currency for each $10 in checking account balances and implies that currency holding is related to deposits by the expression $C = cD = .1D$.

t	be the public's preferred ratio of time deposits (T) to checkable deposits. $t = T/D$.
r	be the reserve ratio for checkable deposits set by the FED.
q	be the reserve ratio for time deposits set by the FED.
e	be the banks' preferred ratio of excess reserves (RE) to checkable deposits; $e=RE/D$. An e of .01 indicates that banks want to keep \$.01 in reserves above the amount required by the FED for each \$1 in checkable deposits.
m	be the public's preferred ratio of [money market mutual funds + savings deposits + overnight repurchase agreements + overnight Eurodollar deposits] to checkable deposits; assume zero reserve ratios on these.
B_o	be the existing amount of monetary base.

6.2.3 FOUR STEP DERIVATION OF THE BASE MULTIPLIERS

The M1 Base Multiplier:

Step 1: **Specify the demand for Base, B^d.** Base demand consists of currency demand, excess reserve demand and required reserves:

$$B^d = C + RE + RR$$

The above assumptions imply $C = cD$, $RE = eD$, $RR = rD + qT$ and $T = tD$, $RR = rD + qtD$ so that base demand is:

$$B^d = cD + eD + rD + qtD = (c + e + r + qt)D$$

Step 2: **Specify the supply of Base, B^s.** Assume the FED can control the supply of Base, the supply is equal to the amount set by the FED, B_o.

$$B^s = B_o$$

Step 3: **Set the supply of base equal to the demand for base and solve for D.**

$B^s = B_d$ or:
$B_o = (c + e + r + qt)D$ and hence
$D = [1/(c + e + r + qt)]B_o$

Step 4: **Use the money supply definition and the last equation to find the final multiplier relation.** For M1:

$$M1 = C + D = cD + D = (1 + c)D$$

using the last two equations together:

$$M1 = [(1 + c)/(c + e + r + qt)]B_o$$

The term $[1/(c + e + r + qt)]$ is the deposit multiplier.

The term $[(1 + c)/(c + e + r + qt)]$ is the M1 base multiplier.

If $c = .5$, $e = .01$, $r = .09$, $q = .05$, $t = 2$, and $B_o = \$600$ billion the base multiplier would be 2.14, and M1 would be $1285.71.

$M1 = [(1 + .5)/(.5 + .01 + .09 + .05(2))]600$
$M1 = [1.5/.7]600 = [2.14]600 = 1285.71.$

The M1 base multiplier of 2.14 indicates that for each $1 increase in the base, the money supply will rise by $2.14.

The M2 base multiplier:

Use the first three steps above and substitute in step four the definition of M2:

Step 4:   M2 $= C + D + T + S + \text{MMF} = cD + D + tD + sD + mD$

$= (1 + c + t + m)D$

M2 $= [(1 + c + t + m)/(c + e + r + qt)]B_o$

Using the same values for the ratios as above and letting $m = 1.5$, we have:

$$M2 = [(1 + .5 + 2 + 1.5)/(.5 + .01 + .09 + .05(2))]600$$
$$M2 = [5/.7]600 = [7.14]600 = 4285.71.$$

Since the M2 multiplier in this example is 7.14, each $1 increase in the base leads to a $7.14 increase in M2.

The nonbank public's portfolio preferences are reflected in the values of c and t; the bank's preferences are reflected in the value of e, and the actions of the FED are reflected in r, q, and B_o.

6.3   DETERMINANTS OF THE MONETARY BASE

6.3.1   THE SOURCES OF THE MONETARY BASE

The following **Supply of Base Equation** is used to calculate the net change in the monetary base. (Shown on the following page). An increase in a positive factor such as the amount of securities held by the FED would cause the monetary base to rise while an increase in a negative factor such as Treasury cash holdings would cause the monetary base to fall.

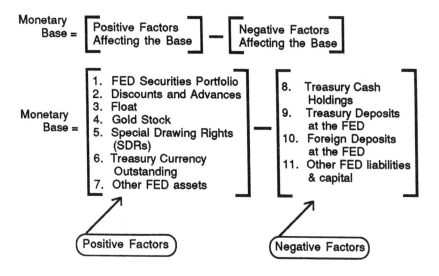

$$\text{Monetary Base} = \left[\begin{array}{l}\text{Positive Factors}\\\text{Affecting the Base}\end{array}\right] - \left[\begin{array}{l}\text{Negative Factors}\\\text{Affecting the Base}\end{array}\right]$$

$$\text{Monetary Base} = \left[\begin{array}{l}\text{1. FED Securities Portfolio}\\\text{2. Discounts and Advances}\\\text{3. Float}\\\text{4. Gold Stock}\\\text{5. Special Drawing Rights}\\\quad\text{(SDRs)}\\\text{6. Treasury Currency}\\\quad\text{Outstanding}\\\text{7. Other FED assets}\end{array}\right] - \left[\begin{array}{l}\text{8. Treasury Cash}\\\quad\text{Holdings}\\\text{9. Treasury Deposits}\\\quad\text{at the FED}\\\text{10. Foreign Deposits}\\\quad\text{at the FED}\\\text{11. Other FED liabilities}\\\quad\text{\& capital}\end{array}\right]$$

Positive Factors   Negative Factors

6.3.2 EXPLANATION OF HOW CHANGES IN THE BASE FACTORS AFFECT THE BASE

FED Securities Holdings

An increase in securities held by the FED increases the base. When the FED buys securities in the open market from government securities dealers, the FED pays for the securities with a check drawn on itself. When the securities dealers deposit the FED check in their commercial banks and the banks send the check to the FED for collection, the FED credits the reserve accounts of the commercial banks by the amount of the check. Since bank reserves are a component of the monetary base, the base rises when the FED buys securities.

Discounts and Advances

When banks borrow from the FED, the FED credits the reserve account of the bank for the amount of the loan, thus increasing the monetary base. Discounts and advances are two forms of borrowing from the FED and are discussed in Chapter 7.

Float:

Float arises in the check collection processing of the FED when the FED credits one bank's reserve account without simultaneously deducting the same amount from the bank on which the check was drawn. For example, suppose Ace Corp. with an account at Chasebank buys $10,000 in supplies from Office Products Inc. by issuing a $10,000 check to Office Products Inc. Office Products deposits the check in Hanovers Bank of New York which sends the check to the FED for collection. At the end of 48 hours, the FED will credit Hanovers Bank's reserve account for $10,000 even if it has not yet been notified by Chasebank that the check is legal and has debited Chasebank's account for $10,000. Since the reserves of Hanovers have risen by $10,000 but the account of Chasebank has not fallen, total reserves and hence the monetary base has increased by the $10,000 in float.

The sum of the first three items in the list of positive factors affecting the float is known as **Federal Reserve Credit** and is among the most important factors affecting the monetary base.

Gold Stock:

The Gold Stock is a short-hand notation for the Gold Certificate Account of the FED. When the Treasury buys $1 billion gold from the public, it writes a $1 billion check drawn on its account at the FED and payable to the seller of the gold. When the check is deposited in commercial banks and collected, the commercial banks will have $1 billion more in reserves and hence the monetary base increases by $1 billion. To finance the purchase of the gold, the Treasury issues a Gold Certificate to the FED for $1 billion and receives in return an increase in Treasury deposits at the FED of $1 billion. Hence when we observe an increase in the Gold Stock (or Gold Certificate Account), we know that the monetary base has increased.

Special Drawing Rights (SDRs)

SDRs are certificates issued by the International Monetary Fund to the Treasury, and by international agreements may be used as the equivalent of gold central banks. Thus, if the Bank of England held $1 billion in dollars that it wanted to have redeemed from the Federal Reserve, rather than exchanging gold for dollars, the FED could redeem the dollars with SDRs (sometimes called "paper gold"). The connection between SDRs and the base is much like that of gold certificates. When the Treasury receives SDRs from the IMF, it exchanges the SDRs for deposits at the FED. If SDRs increase by the same amount as Treasury deposits at the FED, the base would be unchanged. However, if SDR certificates at the FED increase by $1 billion and the Treasury deposits at the FED are unchanged, it must mean that the Treasury wrote $1 billion in checks that resulted in increases in bank reserves and hence in the monetary base.

Treasury Currency Outstanding

This item refers to currency printed or minted by the U.S. Treasury that is in the hands of the public or banks. Since currency (whether issued by the Treasury or the FED) is a part of the base, an increase in Treasury Currency Outstanding must mean an increase in the monetary base. Note: currently, the FED issues nearly all currency, but at one time the Treasury issued paper money as well as coins.

Treasury Cash Holdings

Treasury Cash Holdings refers to the amount of currency held by the Treasury. Given the total quantity of currency issued, if the Treasury holdings rise, it must be true that the combined holdings of currency by the public and the base have fallen and thus the base must have fallen. Thus a rise in Treasury Cash Holdings implies a decrease in the monetary base.

Treasury Deposits at the FED

Another key factor affecting the base is the fiscal activity of the U.S. Treasury. Frequently, when the Treasury writes checks to pay federal employees or to buy supplies, the Treasury's checks are drawn on the Treasury's account at the FED (listed as #9, "Treasury Deposits at the FED", in the list of negative factors above). When the Treasury checks are deposited by employees in their commercial bank accounts, the commercial banks send the checks to the FED for collection, and the FED credits the commercial bank reserve accounts and debits the Treasury's. The credit to the commercial bank reserve account at the FED increases the base; hence, the decline in the Treasury Deposits at the FED is associated with an increase in the base. The opposite effect occurs when the Treasury receives checks from taxpayers and sends the checks to the FED for collection. In this case the FED debits the commercial banks' reserve accounts thus reducing the base.

Foreign Deposits at the FED

Foreign Deposits at the FED are deposits belonging to foreign governments. If a foreign government deposits at the FED $4 billion in checks drawn on U.S. banks, the reserves of the banks will fall when the FED debits their accounts and credits the accounts of the foreign governments. Hence, an increase in Foreign Deposits at the FED results in a decline in the monetary base.

Example of Multiple Transactions on the Base

If the FED buys $1 million in Treasury bills, commercial banks reduce their borrowing from the FED by $.5 million, and Treasury Deposits at the FED fall by $2 million, the base will rise by $2.5 million. Using the base formula, we have:

$$\Delta \text{Base} = \{[\Delta \text{Positive Factors}] - [\Delta \text{Negative Factors}]\}$$
$$= \{[+\$1 \text{ million} - \$.5 \text{ million}] - [-\$2 \text{ million}]\}.$$

6.4 SHIFTS IN THE MONEY SUPPLY

Since the supply of money equals the product of the base multiplier and the monetary base, the money supply curve will increase from M^s_0 to M^s_1 in Figure 6.1 if either the base or the base multiplier increases. For example, if the base multiplier is 2 and the supply of base is $300 and then increases to $325, the money supply will rise from $600 to $650 as in Panel A of Figure 6.1. If the base is $300 and the base multiplier rises from 2 to 2.1, the money supply rises from $600 to $630 as illustrated in Panel B of Figure 6.1.

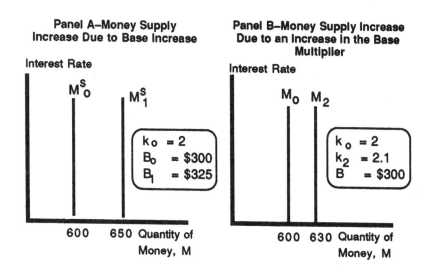

FIGURE 6.1–Money Supply Increases

94

Increases in the monetary base result from increases in the positive factors or decreases in the negative factors in the Supply of Base equation above. Changes in the base multiplier result from changes in the ratios in the multiplier expression such as those in Table 6.2.

Table 6.2
Increases in the M1 Base Multiplier Result From Changes in the Following Ratios

Decrease in	r
Decrease in	c
Decrease in	e
Decrease in	t
Decrease in	q

The money supply curves shown in Panel A of Figure 6.2 are based on the assumption that the ratios in Table 6.2 do not vary as interest rates vary. In practice, these ratios do vary slightly as interest rates change. An increase in the rate of interest on money market securities, such as Treasury bills,

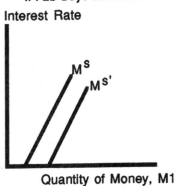

Panel A–Money Supply Varying Positively with the Interest Rate Rotates Rightward if r or q Are Reduced by the FED

Interest Rate

Quantity of Money, M1

Panel B–Money Supply Varying Positively with the Interest Rate Shifts Rightward if FED Buys Securities

Interest Rate

Quantity of Money, M1

FIGURE 6.2

would likely lead to a rise in c, a fall in e, and a fall in t, with a probable net effect of a rise in the quantity of money supplied. As will be explained in Chapter 7, an increase in money market rates will usually result in an increase in the amount of bank borrowing from the FED and thus the amount of monetary base and the money supply. While these effects appear to be small, it is more accurate to view the money supply function as being positively related to market rates as M^s in Figure 6.2. Decreases in r or q and increases in securities holdings by the FED would produce a movement in M^s to $M^{s'}$.

CHAPTER 7

THE FEDERAL RESERVE SYSTEM: STRUCTURE AND TOOLS

The Federal Reserve System (FED) was founded in 1913 by Congress with the intent of providing a means of stabilizing a banking system that had suffered from periodic waves of bank failures and fraud. The numerous times the FED is mentioned in the previous chapters hints at the critical role the institution plays in the economy. The FED carries out three major kinds of activities:

Supervises and Regulates Many Commercial Banks.

Provides Bank Services to Depository Institutions and the Treasury.

Conducts Monetary Policy.

This chapter will provide an overview of the structure of the FED and then examine the major tools that the FED can use to conduct monetary policy.

7.1 STRUCTURE OF THE FEDERAL RESERVE SYSTEM

The main elements of the Federal Reserve are indicated in Figure 7.1. The Board of Governors (seven persons nominated by the U.S. president and confirmed by the Senate for 14 year terms) acts as the executive body of the system. The Board supervises twelve district Federal Reserve Banks which in turn supervise, regulate, and provide services to member banks and, to a lesser degree, other depository institutions as discussed in Chapter 4. Fears of centralized financial power and regional factionalism led Congress to create a set of regional banks rather than a single central bank. However, the system has evolved into what is in fact a central banking authority headed

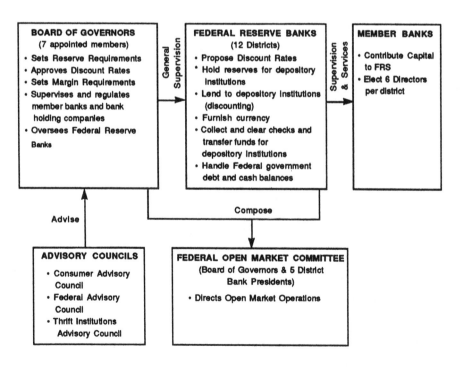

FIGURE 7.1–Structure of the Federal Reserve System

by the Board of Governors (hereafter referred to as "the Board") located in Washington, D.C., and the Board is in turn heavily influenced by its chairman, who is chosen by the president for a four year term. While member banks purchase stock in their district Federal Reserve Banks, this provides only nominal ownership. The member banks earn a fixed 6% return on their stock and vote on six of the nine directors of the district banks. The other three directors are appointed by the Board.

In addition to its supervision of district Federal Reserve Banks, the Board wields several important tools of monetary policy:

It sets reserve requirements within limits set by Congress.

It sets the margin requirement.

It reviews and determines discount rates.

It fills 7 of the 12 seats on the Open Market Committee.

These tools will be discussed in detail below.

The primary monetary policy tool of the district banks is the discount rate. The directors of the district banks propose discount rates to the Board, which approves or rejects the proposals. The **discount rate** is the rate the FED charges depository institutions when they borrow from the FED. Federal Reserve Banks perform a number of the supervisory functions involved in bank regulation and also provide a number of services including the following:

Distribute currency.

Clear checks.

Transfer funds between reserve accounts of depository institutions.

Do research on local and national economic conditions.

Issue and redeem much of the federal debt for the Treasury.

7.2   RESERVE REQUIREMENTS

7.2.1   CURRENT STRUCTURE OF RESERVE REQUIREMENTS

Reserve requirements set by the Federal Reserve Board are applicable to all depository institutions: commercial banks, mutual savings banks, savings and loan associations, credit unions, agencies, and branches of foreign banks in the U.S. The current requirements are given in Table 7.1. The reserve requirements on transactions accounts are based on the average level of deposits over a two week period ending on a Monday. The actual reserves that may be used to satisfy the reserve requirements are based on the average level of reserves over a two week period ending on a Wednesday (with some exceptions).

Table 7.1
Reserve Requirements of Depository Institutions

Deposit Type and Interval*	Reserve Ratio (%)
Net transactions accounts: #	
$0 – $41.5 million	3
Over $41.5 million	12
Nonpersonal time deposits:	
By original maturity	
Less than 1.5 years	3
1.5 years or more	0
Eurocurrency liabilities	
All types	3

* The first $3.4 million of reservable liabilities has a reserve ratio of 0%.

\# MMDA and similar accounts that limit transactions to 6 transfers (of which 3 may be checks) per month are not considered transactions accounts.

7.2.2 USE OF RESERVE REQUIREMENTS TO CONTROL THE MONEY SUPPLY

Reserve requirements can be varied in order to change the money supply. As shown in Chapter 6, increases in the reserve ratio decrease the base multiplier and would hence lower the amount of money generated by the banking system. If the reserve ratio were raised to 1 for deposits, the deposit multiplier could reach, at a maximum, a value of 1. Because such a low multiplier would reduce the variability of the money supply, some economists have advocated the 100% reserve requirement. However, since such a change would reduce bank profits and lending, it is unlikely to be implemented.

At the other extreme, others have advocated a 0% reserve ratio because it would increase bank profits and lending. Since this would greatly increase the base multiplier and thus increase the variability of the money supply, the proposal has little prospect of being adopted. The lower the required reserve ratio is, the higher the base multiplier. Thus, any errors in controlling the monetary base would have a larger impact on the money supply when the required reserve ratio is lower and hence the base multiplier is higher.

While varying the reserve ratios to control the money supply has the advantage of having an immediate effect on all depository institutions in the economy, some consider such changes undesirable because the cost of administering and responding to reserve ratio changes is high. Some have argued that changes in the reserve ratio are undesirable because the impact of a reserve ratio change would be very large. This argument presumes, however, that the change is of the magnitude of about .1. In principle, the changes in the reserve ratio could be made small enough to have any desired impact on the money stock.

Another proposal for using reserves as a tool for controlling economic activity is to pay interest on bank reserves. If the FED wished to restrain bank lending, it would pay a higher rate on reserves and thus induce banks to maintain more excess reserves and thus lend less and create fewer deposits. In times of high unemployment, the FED could pay a very low rate and thus induce banks to use the reserves to accumulate higher earning assets and thus create more loans and deposits. While this is an appealing proposal to bankers, it has not garnered much support elsewhere.

7.3 DISCOUNTING AND ADVANCING

7.3.1 THE DISCOUNT RATE

The second major tool of the FED for influencing economic activity is lending to depository institutions in the form of **discounts and advances**. The term discount refers to cases where the FED purchases a loan made by the commercial bank at a discount from the value of the loan. If the discount rate were 10% (15%), the FED would pay the bank 90% (85%) of the value of the loan. Most lending by the FED is in the form of an advance in which the FED makes a loan which is supported by collateral – usually government securities. Borrowing from the FED is usually called discounting even if technically it is an advance. The rate charged by the FED in advances is also called the **discount rate**. The discount rate is usually less than money market interest rates.

7.3.2 THE SUPPLY OF BORROWED RESERVES

The FED supplies depository institutions with borrowed funds under three programs:

Extended Credit for Exceptional Circumstances –applies in emergency cases when an institution has used all alternative sources and cannot meet liquidity needs over a longer period of time. This program deals with failing banks and regional problems, such as a natural disaster.

Extended Credit for Seasonal Needs – applies for relatively small institutions that face substantial seasonal needs that cannot be readily provided for by market sources of funds without disrupting the normal portfolio of the institution.

Adjustment Credit – loans advanced for short periods of time to help institutions meet needs that are not reasonably satisfied by market sources. These loans are for a maximum of fourteen days and are intended to meet unexpected and temporary liquidity needs.

The last program is the major aspect of monetary policy that is normally referred to when discussing discounting. The FED views **discounting as a privilege and not a right** that is intended for temporary liquidity needs. The FED deems the following as **inappropriate reasons for borrowing**:

to substitute for normal sources of funds.

to substitute for capital.

to support loan or investment expansion.

to take advantage of the differential between market and discount rates.

The FED as a Lender of Last Resort: In times of financial distress, the FED stands ready to provide liquidity that markets cannot supply, thus stabilizing the financial system.

7.3.3 THE DEMAND FOR BORROWED FUNDS

For institutions adhering to the FED's rules, adjustment borrowing would take place for brief periods in which providing for unusual liquidity needs by normal portfolio management would have an unduly severe impact on the institution's portfolio. However, because the institutions are presumably profit maximizing firms and because the discount rate is typically below rates paid by institutions to attract funds, **there is a profit incentive to borrow from the FED.** At times when the **spread** (difference between a market rate, such as the federal funds rate, and the discount rate) is large, borrowing from the FED is also large; this may be considered evidence that profit based discounting takes place even though the FED examines loan requests to see if the criteria for borrowing are met.

7.3.4 THE IMPACT OF DISCOUNT RATE CHANGES

Do changes in the discount rate cause changes in market rates? It is frequently asserted in the press that a reduction in the discount rate will reduce market rates because the discount rate is the cost of borrowing from the FED by depository institutions. It is alleged that such a decline in the cost of borrowing would lead banks to reduce their rates. Because discounting provides only a temporary sources of funds and provides a very small amount of funds to the depository institutions, changes in the discount rate have a minuscule direct impact on bank credit costs. Further, an examination of movements of market rates and discount rates shows that the discount rate follows, rather than leads, market rates. However, there is an **announcement effect** when the FED announces changes in discount rates. That is, typically, on the day after a discount rate is changed, market rates move at least temporarily in the same direction as the discount rate because investors take the announcement as a signal of FED monetary policy. Hence, if the FED announces an increase in the discount rate, the market may view this as a signal that the FED intends to tighten monetary policy and raise interest rates.

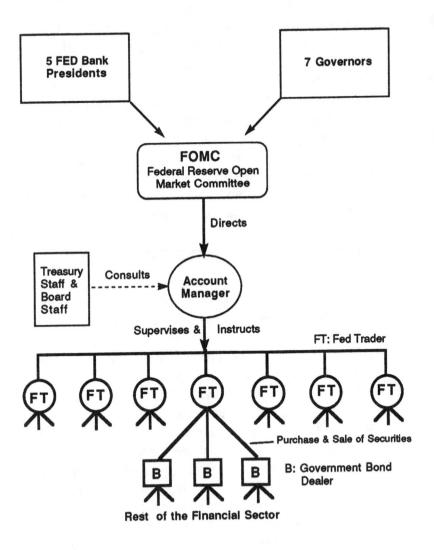

FIGURE 7.2–Persons Involved in Open Market Operations

7.4 OPEN MARKET OPERATIONS

Open market operations consist of the purchasing and selling of securities (normally, just Treasury securities) by the Federal Reserve System. As Figure 7.2 indicates, the Federal Open Market Committee (**FOMC**), a part of the Federal Reserve System, is responsible for open market operations. The FOMC, comprised of five FED presidents and the seven FED governors, meets about every six weeks to determine the policy guidelines for the next 6-8 weeks to be followed by the **account manager**, who is responsible for the day-to-day implementation of FOMC policy. Each day the account manager determines what and how many securities to purchase based on the following:

The FOMC directive.

Statistical projections of reserves and the money supply by the manager's staff at the New York Federal Reserve Bank.

Statistical projections of reserves and the money supply by the staff of the Board of Governors.

Treasury estimates of its receipts and expenditures for the day.

Discussions with government securities dealers.

Discussions with a subcommittee of the FOMC.

The objective of the account manager is to buy and sell securities so that the resulting change in the monetary base will lead to the targeted money supply measures and interest rates. Open market operations aimed at offsetting undesired changes in the base due to factors such as the collection of taxes by the Treasury are **defensive open market operations. Dynamic open market operations** are purchases and sales designed to increase or decrease the base so as to hit policy targets, such as

106

the money supply specified by the FOMC. As the analysis in Chapter 6 illustrated, an open market purchase increases the monetary base and the money supply unless there is an offsetting change in the other factors affecting the base or an offsetting change in the base multiplier. Given the demand for money, an open market purchase should produce lower interest rates, as the money supply increases.

Frequently, the account manager will view the changes in the base to be countered with defensive open market operations as temporary and will use a repurchase agreement rather than a straight purchase of securities. The **repurchase agreement** (repo) occurs when the FED buys the securities and under the agreement the seller will repurchase the securities at a later date at a specified price. The opposite to this arrangement is the **reverse repo or matched sale-purchase**, which is intended to temporarily drain reserves from the banking system and thus temporarily reduce the monetary base.

7.5 MARGIN REQUIREMENTS

The final quantitative tool employed by the FED is the **margin requirement**, which determines the maximum percent of a stock purchase that must be paid for with cash, rather than credit. If the margin requirement is 70%, the purchaser must pay 70% of the price of a stock with cash and, hence, may borrow only 30% of the funds in order to buy the stock. Regulation T of the Federal Reserve Act provides the FED with the authority to set margin requirements for loans by brokers for the purchase of stock and Regulation U provides the authority to set margin requirements for bank loans for stock purchases. Between January 3, 1974 and the present date, the margin requirements have been unchanged at 50%.